G. W. H. LAMPE

Christian, Scholar, Churchman

A MEMOIR BY FRIENDS

G. W. H. LAMPE

Christian, Scholar, Churchman

A MEMOIR BY FRIENDS

Edited by
C. F. D. Moule

MOWBRAY
LONDON & OXFORD

Copyright © A. R. Mowbray & Co. Ltd 1982

ISBN 0–264–66864–2

First published 1982
by A. R. Mowbray & Co. Ltd
Saint Thomas House, Becket Street
Oxford, OX1 1SJ

British Library Cataloguing in Publication Data

G. W. H. Lampe
  1. Lampe, G. W. H.   2. Theologians
  —Great Britain—Biography
  I. Moule, C. F. D.
  209'.2'4   BX5199.L/

  ISBN 0-264-66864-2

(By request, all royalties will be donated
to Addenbrookes Hospital, Cambridge, towards
their Cancer Scanner Fund.)

Typeset by Cotswold Typesetting Ltd
Printed in Great Britain by
Biddles Ltd, Guildford, Surrey

Cover photograph by Dumbleton Studios Ltd, Cambridge

And God said: The day shall dawn
To bring a flower, newly born;
From thy stem in fulness growing
In fragrance sweet, night and morn,
All my people shall adorn,
With breath of life bestowing.
Alleluia, alleluia, alleluia.

From Arthur Honegger's 'King David',
sung at the Memorial Service for
G. W. H. Lampe in the Church of St Mary the Great,
Cambridge, on 18 October 1980.

CONTENTS

vii

CONTENTS   ix

FOREWORD

Literally and metaphorically a man of stature, Professor Lampe was
very much more than the pedant that a professional academic is
popularly imagined to be. Although he had indeed a formidable
battery of learning, the guns did not stick out. Nobody could have
worn his learning more lightly or more modestly, and technical
knowledge was always kept by him firmly in its place as a servant
and not a master. It was his large-hearted humanity that struck all
who met him, and he was as much at home with simple, unlettered
friends as with academic colleagues, and much more concerned to
apply his theology to the demands of the kingdom of God, whether
pastorally or in the councils of the Church, than to shine as a
scholar. Though intolerant of inaccuracy or mediocrity in those
who should know better, he was the most genial and forbearing
companion and the wittiest of raconteurs, and brought enjoyment
with him wherever he went. He was influential far beyond the
classroom or the study, and was listened to with respect whenever
he rose to speak.

This is not a biography but a series of portraits drawn by
observers of various periods and from a variety of different angles.
To be asked to edit such a memoir of Geoffrey Lampe was to be
offered a high privilege but also a daunting task. How could
anybody discharge it adequately? I can only say that I have been
fortunate in the contributors, who have freely given their time and
skill and loving care, and I hope that the total effect of what they
have written will be an authentic impression of a great and greatly
loved man. His wife Elizabeth, herself an essential part of the
portrait, has lent her help and advice without stint at every stage,
and to her is owed in particular the enlisting of friends who could
tell of Geoffrey in the war period. In view of the hosts of friends
eager to do honour to his memory, it would have been easy to
assemble three or four times as many chapters; but my aim was,

1

with few exceptions, to let a single voice speak for each of the main periods or aspects of a life which was more versatile and varied than his mainly academic appointments might suggest to one who did not know him. I can only apologise to any who feel that they ought to have been included in the team but were not.

The structure of the memoir is mainly chronological and explains itself. Its proportions are uneven because, while each contributor was given a 'ceiling' which must not be passed, no 'floor' was specified, and there seemed to be no merit in artificially equalising the pieces. That the Cambridge section is much the longest is due not merely to its being the most recent and thus the most easily documented, but also to the fact that Geoffrey Lampe's willing shoulders seemed to be loaded with more and more responsibilities the longer he lived.

The final section of this book is made up from shorter contributions and from phrases out of letters, reflecting the more intimate and personal side of Geoffrey Lampe's life and character and the supreme courage with which he faced death, living, for four years, on time that he knew was borrowed, with, if possible, greater zest and cheerfulness than ever, and resigning his mortal life at last with a calm contentment that brought peace to others. Where it has been felt necessary, linking material has been inserted between the various contributions and this is indicated by the use of italic type within square brackets.

The following bare outline of his life will serve to locate and explain the contributions.

Geoffrey William Hugo Lampe was born on 13 August 1912, and died on 5 August 1980, a few days before his 68th birthday. His father, who came from Alsace, with forbears from Utrecht, had been a successful conductor of the Bournemouth Symphony Orchestra, but left England before the outbreak of the 1914–18 War, and Geoffrey was brought up by his wonderful mother who lived to see him become Ely Professor of Divinity at Cambridge. He went to Blundell's School and then, with a scholarship, to Exeter College, Oxford, where he had a first-class record in both Greats and Theology Schools. He had chosen Theology because, by then, it was clear to him that he should seek Holy Orders, and he went for training to the Queen's College, Birmingham, whence, in 1937, he was ordained deacon. After a short curacy at Okehampton (1937–8), he became an assistant master at King's School,

Canterbury, marrying Enid Elizabeth Roberts from Tiverton in 1938. In 1941, after the School had been evacuated to Cornwall, he joined up as an Army Chaplain. Attached to the 34 Tank Brigade he took part in the Normandy landings and, in the fighting that followed, was awarded the Military Cross for conspicuous gallantry. The end of the fighting found him a prominent figure among those representing the Church of England in recruiting for the ordained ministry from among the ex-service men. Before demobilisation he had, in 1943, been elected into a Fellowship as Chaplain of St John's College, Oxford. It was from there that, in 1953, he went to Birmingham to occupy the Edward Cadbury Chair of Theology (1953–9). There he also became Dean of the Faculty of Arts (1955–9) and Vice-Principal of the University (1957–60). He held an honorary canonry of Birmingham Cathedral from 1957 to 1959. From 1959 to 1971 he held the Ely Chair of Divinity at Cambridge, with the residentiary canonry at Ely that went with it; and then the Regius Chair from 1971 till retiring age in 1979. He was made an Honorary Canon of Ely on surrendering his residentiary canonry there. In 1963 he became a Fellow of the British Academy. In 1976 he was made an Honorary Fellow of St John's College, Oxford. A DD of Oxford (1953) and of Cambridge by incorporation, he was given honorary doctorates at Edinburgh (1959) and at Lund (1965). In 1978 the King of Sweden created him a Commander of the Northern Star.

The contributions to this memoir show something of the distinction with which he discharged these and other functions, the zest and kindness with which he lived, and the superb courage with which, many times, he faced death. His wife Elizabeth was the ideal partner, entering into each phase of his life with equal whole-heartedness and imaginative understanding and supporting him with a heroism matching his own in days of pain and foreboding. They were devoted to their two children and their spouses, and it was a harmonious and united family.

There is a careful bibliography of Professor Lampe's publications compiled by Dr George Newlands, in G. W. H Lampe, *Explorations in Theology*, *8*, edited by George Newlands (SCM 1981), pp. 138 ff. The following additions may be noted (some suggested by Dr Newlands himself):

'Church Tradition and Ordination of Women', *ExpT* 76, 1964–5, 123–5.

'Diakonia in the Early Church' in J. I. McCord and T. H. L. Parker edd. *Service in Christ, essays for Karl Barth,* Epworth Press 1966, 49–64.

'Secularization in the New Testament and the Early Church', *Theology* 71, 1968, 163–75.

'The Saving Work of Christ, in N. Pittenger ed. *Christ for us Today,* SCM 1968, 141–53.

Is Christianity Credible?, Epworth Press 1981, 28–36.

'The 1938 Report in Retrospect', Introduction to the re-issue of *Doctrine in the Church of England* (SPCK 1982, ix–lx).

'Athens and Jerusalem: joint witnesses to Christ?' in B. Hebblethwaite and S. Sutherland edd. *The Philosophical Frontiers of Christian Theology: Essays presented to D. M. MacKinnon,* Cambridge: University Press 1982, 12–38.

C.F.D.M.

1

GEOFFREY, THE FRIEND

by The Reverend Canon W. Purcell, MA

Canon Purcell was at Keble College, Oxford, while Geoffrey Lampe was at Exeter. Their paths merged for the first time at the Queen's Theological College, Birmingham, where both had gone prior to Ordination. After serving in various parishes in the north and in Kent, Canon Purcell was appointed Head of BBC's Religious Broadcasting in their Midland Region in 1953, in which capacity he was closely associated with Geoffrey in numerous broadcasts in sound and television. Canon Purcell was a Canon of Coventry Cathedral, and subsequently Residentiary Canon of Worcester Cathedral. Now retired from the active Ministry, he is Literary Adviser to a publishing firm.

On an autumn evening during Geoffrey's time at Cambridge he had occasion to go along to the Polytechnic to enrol himself for a course in Russian, with which language he sought some acquaintance preparatory to a visit. But a difficulty emerged: he had no 'O' Levels. This matter was discussed for some time. Eventually, however, the helpful course enroller agreed to overlook the deficiency. Geoffrey thanked him warmly and then, as we walked home, said: 'He was perfectly right, you know'.

But it was very much in character with him to enjoy the mild private joke, and to chuckle over it as he walked, the long overcoat he had had specially made for winter wear flapping round his legs, and his bald head gleaming in the street lights.

That head, even then tending to baldness, impressed me greatly at our first meeting, on another autumn evening, long ago. It was the first day of term, 1936, in the Queen's Theological College, Birmingham. The head seemed perfectly formed, with a great depth of brow. The brown eyes seemed kindly, the expression of the face a curious mixture of uncertainty and amusement, as of someone not quite knowing where he was. But it was impossible not to feel then, as always afterwards, during a friendship which lasted almost half a century, that here was a man of rare qualities. At Queen's, of course, he had by no means developed the poise which came to him in later years. He was not even sure of himself. And some of the eccentricities which were to endear him to many in after-times were already beginning to appear. He was forgetful. He was much attracted by trains, and it was something, in those days of steam, to see him running towards a bridge at the approach of a rising plume in order to stand above as the locomotive passed beneath. Also productive of a lasting memory was the sight of him on the football field, wildly out of place and totally inept at the game, at some match against one of the Selly Oak Colleges.

But there was another impression he gave then which was very strong and proved very persistent. It was of being, without any extravagances of word or deed, a rather holy man. This was infinitely encouraging to any who, struggling upon the road of faith, were finding the going hard. So to see Geoffrey kneeling in the chapel at Queen's, very concentrated, was to feel rather as some testified in an earlier day to feeling about William Temple—that, if this road was possible for him, then surely it ought to be for lesser mortals, also. It was possible to touch upon this same point nearly half a century later when, at a service at Great St Mary's, Cambridge, to celebrate Geoffrey and Elizabeth's fortieth wedding anniversary, it was my privilege to be the speaker. I recalled then, as I do now, some words written as graffiti on the walls of the men's washroom at the Round House Theatre, London, on the first night of that once celebrated musical, *Godspell*: 'If you aren't part of the solution, you must be part of the problem'. The point sought to be made was that Geoffrey, as regards the baffling problems of human life and of faith, always ultimately seemed part of the solution.

One difficulty, however, in writing of him in any capacity—and I write simply as a friend—is that there were so many sides to him that the entirety of him tends to elude the grasp. The diversity of his concerns, as well as the distinction of his contributions to them, are apparent in the pages of this book. But where is the whole man? What kind of a character stood at the centre of all this variegated excellence? The climber who said that it was very difficult to say what Everest looked like because appearances depend upon the angle of approach was expressing a difficulty which can also arise when the need is to describe a very large personality. So it is with Geoffrey. It may be that it is not now possible to see all of him. Perhaps, indeed, it never was. All one can do is to say what one did see within the context of a friendship which, for some reason or other, he seemed to find agreeable and I found an inestimable and unforgettable privilege.

It was a friendship which took the form of many walks and many talks. And, when we stayed in each others houses, it was rarely that we did not 'hear the chimes at midnight'. Some of the things Geoffrey said, and some of the stories he told, I noted down at the time, and to look them up now is to recall happy memories of such pleasant occasions. Some, of course have dated. Others are private. But a few, here and there in this curious collection, have some importance in being revealing of aspects of his character not always readily discernible in his public image.

There was, for instance, his sense of humour, which stood in very close relationship to that particular taste for the absurd or ridiculous which seems to grow in the soil of Oxford or Cambridge. Thus Geoffrey relished telling of how, during his time as an army chaplain, he and another uniformed representative of that branch of the Service were relieving the boredom of a long railway journey by speculating on how possible, or otherwise, it would be to sleep in the luggage racks. To settle the question, each climed on to a rack, one on each side of the compartment, and so remained until a ticket collector entered. Or there was the time when Geoffrey's tank brigade was returning from manoeuvres in southern England. He, charged with the task of finding men accommodation as night fell, was vastly diverted to find a boys' preparatory school, where he was turned down, and almost out, by a very small and indignant school master whose patriotism was not equal to the occasion. An equally prosperous neighbour, however, was better disposed and took them in. But two embarrassments remained: she annoyed the Brigadier by calling him 'General', and bringing him port at unsuitable hours, and the local vicar protested that the soldiery were cooking on his tombstones, which they were. Geoffrey also enjoyed the memory of how, when the brigade next day retreated through a neighbouring town, the population came out to cheer them, thinking they were the second front.

But there was, of course, always another side to this. He once in after-times illustrated what he meant by trust in a God whom one could not see, and sometimes did not seem able to experience, by a memory from these same chaplain days. Apparently his duties had included acting as an inert body on a stretcher during night exercises involving medical personnel. He said, 'You didn't know where you were going; the night would be dark; you were helpless; all you had to rely on were strong arms bearing you up. But they never let you down'.

He liked also, when he could be persuaded to talk about his chaplain days at all, which was not very often, to speak of an encounter with a squadron of flame-throwing tanks. It struck him as agreeably comic that the Commander of one of these fearsome machines, a gentle youth, turned out to be a former classical sixth form boy from King's, Canterbury, and an ordination candidate who had consulted Geoffrey as to what to read at Oxford. A cross-check on this story came to me after the war when I encountered this same young man. He said that he and Geoffrey in fact met in a slit trench under mortar fire, upon which occasion Geoffrey said, 'Good morning, Watson. I believe the last time we met was during the Peloponnesian War'.

I had, as it happened, a personal glimpse of him during those army days of which others will be able to write much more fully. It was in the summer of 1945 that Geoffrey invited me to go out as a speaker to a retreat and conference house which he was running for the Army Chaplains' Department on what was then the 30 Corps District of the British Zone in Germany. It was a rather strange situation. There were displaced persons in the woods, there was a frightened local population around. The Red Army was not far away. Yet in the house was a very Anglican Free Church conference retreat in progress. Geoffrey, as Warden, was in command. So there he stood in the hall-way, wearing his MC ribbon, welcoming his young khaki guests, men and women, with that particular courtesy he had for the young. But of his authority there was no doubt.

Indeed, his power of command was always very considerable. Thus in argument—and we had many of them—it was usually evident that he held his views to be correct. And though he never enforced it with discourtesy, he was prepared to maintain, by patient and lengthy development of his case, what he felt to be the essential rightness of it. It would be untrue to say that he was obdurate. It might be truer to say that he felt that, while patience was necessary to cope with a differing view, a lucid development of the truth of his own would always prevail. No doubt this made him a formidable debater in some of the big issues which came to be among his concerns as the years went by. It could make him formidable, too, in smaller things. Thus, on some of the long walks which we so much enjoyed, if a question arose as to the route, he would demonstrate from the map the correct one, patiently dispose of any objections, and then set off. It was usually best to follow, because it led to the right destination in the end.

Of Geoffrey's many kindnesses others may speak; of his notable academic achievements others will speak. But there was one incident of which, because it was of such importance to him at the time and afterwards, and also because it was an outcome of our friendship, I feel I must speak.

On 18 April 1965, Easter Day, Geoffrey preached at the morning Eucharist in St Martin's, Birmingham Parish Church. The service was televised nationally by the BBC. On the evening of the same day, in nearby studios, excerpts from the recording of the sermon were shown, and a group of people from the morning's congregation questioned him as to what he had said. This programme was presented under the title 'The Empty Tomb'. 'If Christ was not raised, then our gospel is null and void, and so, is your faith. . . . But the truth is, Christ was raised to life.' After that came the question: 'What are we to make of this today? How far is the resurrection story still credible and how much does it matter?'

In view of the immense furore which followed it is worth recalling what exactly Geoffrey did say during the morning sermon. He began:

'When Paul wrote these words he was face to face with a crisis of belief: the crisis . . . in which we also stand. One thing there was that he held on to: a fixed conviction that a man who had been executed, who was dead and buried, was alive now, a living person: that, so far from that man's death being the end of him, he was Paul's own Lord and Master, the one whom he must follow, trust in, and obey if his life was to have any meaning.

'How could Paul believe anything so fantastic? Because he was absolutely convinced that Jesus, who had been sentenced to death by Paul's own friends for reasons of which he thoroughly approved, had encountered him personally with shattering effect. For that experience had turned his whole life and all its values upside down. It had made him devote the rest of his life, at the cost of immense risk and suffering, to the one task of spreading the good news: that God had said "Yes" to Jesus; that his way of life had been vindicated; that what he did and said had been true after all; that love, understanding, forgiveness, self-sacrifice are the real things that matter in the end.'

There are two other passages from this sermon which may be quoted because they shed some light on what happened in the evening programme. After having briefly described the Damascus road experience of Paul, Geoffrey continued: 'For Paul . . . Jesus became a living reality, and, for ever after, that was the one thing that really mattered . . . That is the Easter story. Forget, if you will, the picture, beloved of the old artists, of a body, holding a flag of triumph, stepping out of a grave. That suggests a corpse come back to life on this physical plane. If that were what the idea of Christ's resurrection means, then it were better forgotten. Such a Christ is dead. He remains buried. The real Christ is not a revived corpse. He lives in the fullness of God's life. He is the life, the truth, the way, for us. He lives for us and in us. For the experience of Easter didn't stop with Peter, Paul and the rest. The living Christ may encounter us too, very often in our relationships with other people. And, for what it may be worth, I know that he has gripped me: in so far as his love compels me to try to follow him, inspires me, encourages me, and forgives me for what I am. . . .

'Easter speaks about God. It is not a story of a return of a dead person to this life. It has nothing in common with what a surgeon might do if he got a heart moving again after it had stopped. It has nothing to do, either, with the idea that there is some part of our being that is inherently immortal: some entity that we might call a soul. No. As far as our human nature is concerned, when you're dead you're dead; and so was Jesus. Still less does Easter say that death is unreal. It's brute fact . . . The Easter experience tells us that God *is*; that faith in God will not let us down; that Jesus's way of life, his trust in a God of love, was justified; that a life of faith in God and so of love and acceptance of other people, was vindicated for him and can be vindicated for us too. God has said the last word about it; and that word is "Yes". God's affirmation of Jesus is stronger than what we foolishly call the real world; it is stronger than death itself. God *is* the God whom Jesus taught us to call "Our Father". He *is* the God of love: love which will not let go, even through death. Here, if we follow Jesus, the living Lord, lies our hope of reaching that perfect relationship with God which, because God is unchanging, we call eternal life.'

This, then, was the sermon upon which the discussion in the evening programme was based. It is difficult indeed to see anything to which exception could possibly be taken. It is equally evident from it how hard Geoffrey tried to simplify, and to keep himself constantly aware that he was addressing a mass audience. The same consideration applied, of course, to the evening transmission; this time on a far greater scale, evening audiences being much larger. What is more, in those days this particular programme was repeated later in the same day so that those who had not been able to view earlier could do so. These included clergy, and it was from among this body that the great majority of Geoffrey's subsequent critics came.

The main thrust of these criticisms was that Geoffrey seemed to have questioned the historical basis of the resurrection narratives. It added to the enormity of it all, in his critics' view, that he had done so on Easter Day itself. But was this true? It was not. I was there, sitting alongside Geoffrey in the studio, and indeed sharing the dicussion which he had with the group of lay people who had been among his morning congregation. This friendly and intelligent group were particularly interested to know what he had to say about what might be called the physical aspects of the resurrection story. Did he, for example,—and this was one of the many questions asked—think it important that an actual discovery of an actually empty tomb was made? What had he to say about the resurrection narratives? Did they represent historical truth, or could they be understood as illustrative of a greater happening—an encounter with the living Christ, as he had said, lying behind them?

With such questions, in the limited time at his disposal, and speaking, as was necessary, entirely extempore, Geoffrey wrestled mightily. He also wrestled, in my humble opinion, entirely successfully. Only one moment in the whole transmission gave some cause for disquiet, and that was when he used the word 'myth' in its theological sense. Whether he realised at the time that it is only too readily, in the public mind, associated with the word 'mythical' I do not know.

But this was what many of his critics thought he had inferred, and they were very angry. I have often thought that perhaps it would have been better not to expose Geoffrey to this very severe test. And I have felt guilty about it because I know that he accepted the invitation to appear in these programmes from me as a friend. However, it was done, and the reaction was very considerable indeed. He received something approaching a thousand letters. Many of these were from people who had been helped and illuminated by what he had said. Others, however, were severely critical, and the shock-wave of the programme continued for some time. Without a doubt, Geoffrey was troubled by some of this reaction. By only one part of it, however, was he angered. A clergyman speaking at a diocesan conference in the North shortly afterwards was reported as having said that the speaker 'should have done his homework better'. This was more than Geoffrey could take, and a somewhat severe correspondence ensued with the author of this unfortunate remark. A more fruitful sequel was the book which Geoffrey subsequently wrote in conjunction with Professor MacKinnon in which were discussed further some of the points which Geoffrey had made in the programme and which widened out into a debate between the two on some aspects of the resurrection.

It may perhaps finally be said about this whole episode that it seems extraordinary now, all these years afterwards, that what he said should have appeared to so many to be so much more radical than it was.

Without a doubt, Geoffrey was always very conscious of the pastoral responsibilities of the theologian—responsibilities which increased in proportion as his theology was in any way radical. This formed the basis of many of the talks which we had, and I like to think that maybe these were of some value to him, in that they presented the opportunity of hearing what an ordinary man had to say. I think for example, that he enjoyed dealing with such rather odd speculative questions, deliberately put to him in order to see what he would have to say, as 'Would it be possible to infer, from the fact that the report *Doctrine in the Church of England* is a great deal longer than the subsequent *Christian Believing* document, that in the opinion of its framers there is now so much less which it is possible to believe?' His answer to that would require considerably more space than is available here. But I am sure he would have agreed with a remark made by Wilfred Knox, in his *St Paul and the Church of the Gentiles*, a book produced in the early thirties when some of what has become today's theological debate was just beginning, that 'if we read a great deal of theology, we shall need a great deal of faith'. I think also that he would have agreed with Penelope Fitzgerald, in her biography *The Knox Brothers*: 'The widening gap between theologians and anyone else to whom Christianity might be of interest was of great concern to him'. That was true of Geoffrey, and it was a concern often reflected in the conversations we had together.

But all friendships are better for a disagreement. A long-standing one between us concerned the place of the mystical, the undefined and undefinable, together with the insights of the artist and the poet in any attempt at reaching out to spiritual truth. If he did not like this approach I think it was because it seemed to him to lack sufficient precision and order. To such a remark that, for example, von Hügel defines a living religion as a tension between the three elements of the institutional, the intellectual, and the mystical, he would reply with one of his smiles that the last of those three did not seem to him sufficiently clear.

I once ventured to say to him, in the course of one of these arguments, that he had a 'Roman mind', in the sense of supposing that, if one could impose a sense of order upon a given problem, then that problem was well on its way to be solved. His reply was that, if such was indeed a definition of a Roman mind, then he would admit to having one. And there we left it.

But not quite. When he came to die it seemed as though he imposed order upon even this last enemy. With deliberation, taking one issue at a time and disposing of it, he so ordered his affairs that, when the time came for him to depart, he was able to do so with a striking composure. It fell to my lot to be called in on the day before he died to discuss some literary matters which he wished dealt with. It was as though death were to be kept waiting until Geoffrey was good and ready. So perhaps he was right, after all, in claiming that a problem was in a fair way to being dealt with when it could be brought to order.

2
EARLY DAYS AT OXFORD

by M. V. Osmond, OBE, MA

Mr Osmond was a close friend of Geoffrey Lampe at Exeter College, Oxford, where he read classics and law. He was called to the Bar in 1938 and was awarded the Poland Prize in criminal law. He joined the Territorial Army on leaving school and in the war served with the Royal Fusiliers and in staff appointments in India. Afterwards he worked for the Council for the Protection of Rural England and on his retirement as Secretary in 1977 was appointed OBE. He is married, with one daughter.

At Exeter College, Oxford, Geoffrey Lampe and I were exact contemporaries. We went up together, he as the senior scholar of the year, in October 1931, and for the next five years we were intimately associated in both work and play. From our first meeting I recognised in him a kindred spirit and our friendship was grounded in a remarkably close community of tastes and interests and opinions. I have therefore some claim not only to be one of his oldest surviving friends but also to have known him during that period better than anyone else.

Exeter was not one of Oxford's largest colleges, nor was it, either academically or athletically, one of the most distinguished; but it was a happy, friendly community, with none of the cliques and social divisions which for us would have spoilt some of the others. The Rector of the college was Dr R. R. Marett, a Jerseyman and a distinguished anthropologist, who ran the college on a light rein and was universally liked and respected, despite—or partly because of—his reputation as a teller of tall stories, to which we soon learnt to add the necessary grains of salt.

The college, needless to say, would have struck today's undergraduates as in some respects a primitive institution. Our rooms were heated by coal fires, we had no running water, and one had to walk through several quadrangles to find either a lavatory or a bathroom. Women visitors were strictly excluded except for limited periods. As for costs, a circular issued by the college to freshmen's parents advised them that an undergraduate living 'with due economy but without privation' would need a sum of £220 per annum to cover all university and college charges (including board and lodging in term-time) and reasonable expenditure on recreational and social activities; and this, in my experience, was a fair estimate. Geoffrey's and my scholarships of £100 per annum therefore made a significant contribution to balancing our budgets.

Our first five terms were devoted to Honour Classical Moderations, under the tuition of Eric Barber, an authority on Propertius. To us freshmen Barber was a somewhat frightening figure, especially when peering with the air of an inquisitor at our Greek and Latin compositions; but he was in fact the kindest of men and, once the ice was broken, we became very fond of him. He later proved a most able successor to Marett as Rector.

In those days attendance at lectures was largely voluntary; tutors merely drew their pupils' attention to those which might prove most helpful. Nevertheless Geoffrey and I were reasonably diligent in attendance, and among the lectures which we remembered with special pleasure were those of Cyril Bailey on Cicero and Lucretius and of Professor Gilbert Murray on Homer, the latter not least because of his wonderfully mellifluous voice. After a few terms we startled Barber by telling him that we were thinking of attending a series of lectures—on Virgil, I believe—by a fellow of one of the women's colleges. This he evidently thought an extraordinary idea, but he raised no objection and from time to time inquired with an amused air how we were getting on with 'the lady'. Unfortunately, her lectures were very dull and attendance dwindled until Geoffrey and I, mainly from motives of chivalry, became the only survivors. At this stage the lecturer, to our relief, decided to discontinue the course, and we sought to console her by inviting her out to coffee.

In our second year Barber, having more confidence in our expertise than we had ourselves, put us in for the Hertford Scholarship. This is an advanced university prize examination of four or five sessions devoted to Latin composition and extremely difficult unseen translation. By way of practice, he gave us some old examination papers on which to flex our muscles, and one of the unseens was a long passage of Plautus full of Latin puns. The mere task of translation was difficult enough; to invent English equivalents for the puns seemed next to impossible. However, we had a fellow-scholar named Tony Schofield (later a Canon of Blackburn), whose wit and verbal dexterity were proverbial, and with him we spent an hilarious evening devising a series of English puns—all the most ingenious being supplied by Schofield, not us. Unfortunately, this was the very passage which the examiners chose to set in the examination, and Geoffrey and I, who were in adjoining seats, looked at each other in consternation, for clearly the more felicitous the English puns, the less they would be appreciated if contributed by two candidates from the same college! Thus it was that we made our nearest approach to an examination cheat. Through a surreptitious exchange of notes we agreed to use our prepared puns alternately throughout the paper, and this we successfully did, filling the gaps as best we could. We neither of us won the scholarship, but the examiners gave me—and, I hope, Geoffrey too—a pure alpha for this particular paper, adding however that they thought the candidate must have seen the passage before!

After Honour Moderations we proceeded to Greats, which, as most readers of this memoir will know, falls (or then fell) into two main parts, philosophy and ancient history. Our tutors in these subjects respectively were William Kneale, a most likeable man whose style of teaching however failed to inspire us, and Dacre Balsdon, whose tutorials were highly entertaining but not, in our view, very useful. We therefore depended greatly on our lectures and these, as might be expected of the Greats school, were of a remarkably high standard. Among the more memorable were those of Lord Franks (as he later became) on moral philosophy, who at the beginning of his two-term course proposed to deal first with the question 'What is the proper subject-matter of moral philosophy?' and at the end of it expressed regret that this preliminary point had not yet been disposed of. Then there were Father D'Arcy (on Aristotle) and E. F. Carritt (on moral philosophy again) whose lectures were brilliantly illuminating and so admirably academic as to give no hint of their personal commitment to Roman

Catholicism and Communism respectively. In modern philosophy I think Geoffrey and I may have treated our studies somewhat light-heartedly, as is perhaps suggested by our joint invention of a new doctrine called Transcendental Negativism, whose basic tenet was 'No universal proposition, even the universal proposition that no universal proposition is valid, is valid'. (This maxim can of course be expanded *ad infinitum*.)

Our life at Oxford was by no means all work and no play, but organised games did not appeal to us. For a few weeks in our first term we joined the college boat club, but the club was not interested in any but serious rowers and for us the sport was far too time-consuming. Thereafter our water-borne expeditions were made by punt or canoe and, in that golden age when in retrospect the summers seem always to have been fine, we spent much time on the Cherwell (then easily navigable by punt as far as Islip) and on the Thames down stream to Abingdon and up stream to Swinford Bridge and Bablock Hythe. We also did a great deal of walking in the Oxford countryside, often extending our range by means of the plentiful train and bus services which were then in operation. Another of our shared interests was archaeology; we were keen members of the University Archaeological Society, and Roman villas and ancient churches and houses provided the focal points of many of our country walks. We also did some digging, under the direction of Dr Leeds, the Keeper of the Ashmolean; but our search for Romano-British 'post-holes' led us to the conclusion that with our sharp-pointed trowels such archaeological evidence was far easier to create than to discover and we did not persist in this activity for long.

At the beginning and end of terms we undertook a number of longer walks, either between Oxford and my home at Bristol by a variety of Cotswold routes or sometimes ranging further afield, sleeping at pubs and cottages or occasionally under haystacks on the way. On one of our happiest end-of-term expeditions we walked beside the Thames from Oxford to its 'official' source at Thameshead near Cirencester and thence followed the Fosse Way to Bath and onwards by cycle to its terminus in South Devon. On all such journeys Geoffrey was a wonderful companion—entertaining, resourceful, considerate and uncannily skilful at map-reading and at finding cross-country footpaths which to others were invisible. Did this training, I wonder, help him in picking his way through the theological tussocks and quicksands of his later life?

Of our leisure interests in Oxford itself little need be said. Like most undergraduates, we went to concerts and dances and theatres and cinemas, including occasional jaunts to the West End, and we belonged to numerous college societies and discussion groups, including the flourishing Church Society.

In political affairs we took only a detached interest and in party terms we followed the undergraduate fashion of the day in standing somewhat to the left of centre. Although this was the period of the 'hunger marches' and Oswald Mosley's Blackshirts (who had some scuffles in Oxford) and the rise of Hitler and the 'King and Country' debate in the Oxford Union (of which we were not members), we engaged in no political activity and viewed all the political parties with a mixture of amusement and suspicion. We had, however, great confidence in Anthony Eden and high hopes for the League of Nations, which with typical undergraduate optimism we expected to intervene wherever world affairs were not going quite to our liking. The Silver Jubilee of King George V we celebrated with enthusiasm, cycling out in the evening to join the local residents in their carousals at a village pub.

In vacation, Geoffrey and I had many splendid holidays together, either on our own or with small parties of Oxford friends. Among the most enjoyable were a camping holiday in Jersey, two visits to Lundy—in one of which Dr Marett was a most welcome member of our party—a walk lasting several days on and around Exmoor, a voyage by paddle steamer from Brighton to Bristol and several holidays at cottages in the Hartland peninsula with our future wives. None of these, I should add, made any pretence of being 'reading parties'; they were all just 'parties'.

Things, I am sure, are very different now, but my recollection is that in the 1930s undergraduates did not worry greatly about their future careers or discuss them with their friends. Certainly Geoffrey and I did not. This may have been partly due to a lingering notion that in an academic atmosphere it was somehow indecent to consider seriously anything so mundane as earning a living; but in our circle there was also the fact that for many of our friends the question was already settled. Several were destined for the Church, some (including me) for a legal career, some for the Civil or Colonial Service, and others for teaching, and these intentions were well known and accepted.

Geoffrey had never told me of his plans; nor had I asked him. I think I imagined that he would probably become a schoolmaster. It therefore came as a complete surprise to me when, after taking a first in Greats, he decided to remain at Oxford for a fifth year and to read the Honour School of Theology with a view to ordination.

Until then we had shared a general interest in religious matters; we enjoyed 'going to church' and did so not only in the College Chapel but in the University Church and other churches in Oxford and the surrounding villages; we both belonged to the college Church Society, which discussed ecclesiastical and religious matters with a visiting speaker; and in 1932 we sat through Canon Streeter's splendid Bampton Lectures on 'The Buddha and the Christ', though I little suspected that my companion was a future Bampton Lecturer himself. Clearly, therefore, we were rather more religiously inclined than many undergraduates, but we spoke little of our personal beliefs, and when in the course of our Greats studies we discussed problems of morals or metaphysics the religious factor was something which we tended to discount or to relegate, as it were, to a footnote. During those years I was never conscious of any deep religious conviction on Geoffrey's part, or indeed of any major difference in this respect—as in so many others—between his position and my own. Still less had I any inkling of his later emergence as an eminent theologian.

Of his fifth-year studies there is little I can say, for I knew no more about his work in the Theology School than he knew of mine in Jurisprudence. Having to cover in less than one year what were normally seven-term courses, we were both hard at work, but our friendship continued and we still met almost daily. In the event, Geoffrey not only took a First in Theology, but—as he told me with an air of embarrassed surprise—was personally congratulated by the examiners on the exceptional quality of his papers.

He then moved on to Queen's College, Birmingham, a broad-based theological college which, as a liberal evangelical, he felt would be more congenial than one of the more sectarian institutions.

At this point our ways parted, and not only in terms of our places of work and residence; for ever since leaving Oxford I have been of an agnostic disposition, and this divergence of outlook between Geoffrey and me grew with the passing years. But it did nothing to impair our friendship and, though he was well aware of my views, he refrained, with characteristic tolerance, from any attempt to proselytise.

Tolerance was indeed one of his most notable virtues, along with absolute sincerity, a splendid sense of humour, great courage, and an equable temperament. In nearly fifty years of close friendship we never had or even approached a quarrel, and I have never known anyone whose company was at once so stimulating and so relaxing. For me, as for many others, this made him

'a safe companion and an easy friend',

and we shall not see his like again.

3

ARMY CHAPLAIN

Between Exeter College, Oxford, and the army days came the period of training for Holy Orders at Birmingham, and then the curacy at Okehampton. Here his friend Mervyn Osmond, the writer of the account of their undergraduate days, once visited him and recalls the confidence and efficiency of one who had only just begun his ministry, and his sociable involvement in the town's activities. Then followed Geoffrey's marriage and the mastership at King's School, Canterbury. This move into the scholastic world after only a year in a parish was presumably due to a sense that this was where his most effective ministry was likely to lie. There is evidence that he had previously applied for a chaplaincy in another school, where he was defeated by a candidate of no intellectual distinction but great athletic prowess.

Some of the most impressive glimpses into his moral stature come from those who knew him as an Army Chaplain. Most of them were oblivious of his distinction as a scholar, which he sedulously concealed. They knew him simply as a brave and kindly man. An NCO recalls his total disregard for distinctions of rank: '... he was a great fellow, very humble. He was somebody, I was nobody, but it made no difference. When there was a show behind the lines, it used to be officers upstairs, other ranks downstairs; but he always made me go with him upstairs ...' Another correspondent draws these two little pictures, one in 1944 before the battle of the Reichwald, and one during it. 'He was lost without his pipe and the weekly ration of tobacco was to him inadequate. He arranged with the Mess Sergeant to save the used tea-leaves and dry them and then to mix a good pile of them with his crumbled up ration. I can see him now kneeling on the floor with a sheet of newspaper in front of him doing his mixing act—and very absorbed in it he was. After a week or so of battle in the bridgehead during which one or other of our regiments was engaged each day, I met him outside a

23

dressing station coming from the wounded. His eyes had sunk back into his head and he was sooty black under the eyes. He had seen awful things and I think he was as badly shocked as the wounded. I made some remark—"You look tired" (or perhaps "awful"), and he smiled wearily. He was suffering yet enduring. As I said . . . he was a good bloke.' Another attended, in Holland, a Communion Service 'which he held for a small group under rather difficult conditions, and the memory of that simple service is always with me . . . He was a wonderful Brigade Padre . . .'

There follow reminiscences from Mr B. H. Wilson, CBE, the late Canon F. Bussby (whose lamented death occurred just as his contribution was being revised), and Canon A. Inglis. It must have been not long before the action here referred to that Geoffrey had a narrow escape. He described it subsequently, in a sermon on providence, and characteristically refused to accept it uncritically as 'providential'.

'I was lying in a very cramped and frighteningly shallow trench, and I was extremely envious of my colleague the doctor, who had got his orderlies and drivers to construct a magnificent dugout, properly roofed, spacious, and deep. During a quiet interval, when I was moving around with the doctor, he invited me to join his party. One of them could easily move from the front of his dugout to the back, leaving room for me. That was exactly what I wanted, but I found myself under a very strange and quite irrational compulsion to tell him I would rather stay where I was. This was no kind of premonition of trouble. But I thought afterwards that I began to understand what those people in the Old Testament may have felt when they said, "God spoke to me and said . . ." An hour or two later one of the big missiles from a multi-barrelled mortar fell in the entrance of the doctor's dugout precisely at the spot I should have been occupying had I accepted his invitation. That looks like an instance of special divine providence. But it clearly wasn't, because if I had followed my natural inclination to seek safety, I should probably have saved the life of the unfortunate man who would then have moved back to make room for me. As it was, my "inner voice" could be said to have resulted in his being blown to pieces, as he literally was.' In the sermon it is argued that 'providence' must be thought of as something much deeper, and in terms of God's creative use of all sorts of complicated circumstances—including both human sin and human responsiveness to him—to work out his purposes.

by B. H. Wilson, CBE, MA

Mr Wilson is a Solicitor and was, until his retirement, a Town Clerk in Local Government. He is now Chairman of the Metropolitan Housing Trust. He was an exhibitioner at Corpus Christi College, Cambridge. In the war, he served with the Royal Armoured Corps, and in 1944 was awarded the MBE. In 1972 he was awarded the CBE. He is married, with one son.

'Padre' Geoffrey Lampe was attached to 34 Tank Brigade, an independent armoured brigade equipped primarily with heavy Churchill tanks. Our role was normally expected to be to support the infantry in 'setpiece' attacks. Shortly before 'D' Day in June 1944 the brigade comprised three regiments, 107 RAC (King's Own Lancaster), 147 RAC (Hampshire) and 153 RAC (Essex). As the senior Church of England chaplain, with the honorary rank of Captain, he divided his time between Brigade Headquarters and the three regiments.

Luckily for 107 RAC, to which I was Technical Adjutant at that time, Geoffrey Lampe spent several weeks leading up to our embarkation for Normandy with my regiment, and the officers at Regimental HQ, of whom I was one, soon struck up a very close friendship with him. We were then stationed at Headley, on the borders of Surrey and Hampshire, not far from Brigade HQ at Hindhead. Most of the daytime was spent waterproofing the tanks in case we had a 'wet' landing on the Normandy beaches, but the evenings in the mess were very pleasant occasions. One or two of us soon discovered that Geoffrey both enjoyed and excelled at a game of bridge. His bridge-playing was typical of his character, his quiet unassuming and friendly manner covering exceptional ability— and he was always most apologetic and surprised when he won!

On the 16 June 1944 we moved down to our embarkation point at Lee-on-Solent and about a fortnight later sailed across the Channel in tank landing ships, and were successfully beached on the Normandy coast. Geoffrey was still with our Regimental HQ when 107 RAC went into action for the first time in the late evening of 15 July. The regiment formed up on the reverse slope of 'Hill 112', a vantage point which had already been bitterly fought over before we arrived. The objective was to capture the hill and put a battalion of the Highland Division into occupation of a small hamlet on the other side, with the singularly inappropriate name of 'Bon Repos'.

Geoffrey, who could well have considered that his proper place during the attack was some way to the rear with the 'soft' supporting vehicles of the regiment, nevertheless decided that he would be more useful with the armoured units of the regiment, although as I remember he was not equipped with any form of armoured vehicle. He felt he 'might be needed' in case there were casualties. The evacuation of casualties was an aspect of war to which we had never paid much attention (perhaps understandably) in our training in England. I suspect that Geoffrey wisely concluded that this might be the case, and as things turned out he was right, and his help in evacuating the wounded was invaluable.

Attacks usually began at 'first light', but to gain an element of surprise this one took place at 'last light', making the whole operation extremely difficult, especially for a unit having its first taste of action. To protect ourselves from the German 88 mm anti-tank guns (which were pretty lethal) a great deal of smoke was put down, which, when added to the gathering gloom as night fell, proved to us the accuracy of the phrase 'the fog of war'. Although the attack was successful and the infantry were able to occupy their new positions at 'Bon Repos', the tanks had the utmost difficulty in finding their way back to the forward rally point where the regiment was expected to rendezvous. My personal task after the attack was to find and arrange for the recovery of any broken down or knocked out tanks, but although I knew there had been some casualties I found it almost impossible to locate them. To add to our difficulties the Germany artillery and mortars had now been fully alerted, and the whole area was being subjected to heavy and continuous shelling. In spite of this Geoffrey Lampe continued with his self-appointed task of helping to evacuate the wounded. I well remember that at about dawn the next morning when I was sitting disconsolately in the comparative safety of my armoured car, there was a tap on the outside. I peered out and there was Geoffrey, standing in the open (though shells were still falling) and asking in quiet and kindly tones if I was 'all right'!

This was the first major action of 107 RAC, but the following day another regiment of the brigade, 147 RAC, was due to make a similar attack with another unit of the Highland Division. Feeling that he ought to be with them Geoffrey typically transferred himself to them, and as far as I know remained with them during the period when the allies finally broke out of the bridge-head and advanced across France. It is presumably during this period that Geoffrey was cited for the Military Cross—an award which, judging by his conduct with us during our first night of action, could never have been more deserved. *[A transcript of the citation follows, on p. 28.]*

During the rest of the fighting in North West Europe, we used to see Geoffrey Lampe from time to time, but as the brigade was doing far more travelling than during our early days in Normandy, he was presumably more often with Brigade HQ.

Since the war 107 RAC, which had earlier combined with 153 RAC (who had suffered severe casualties) to form one unit, regularly had a regimental dinner at the Charing Cross Hotel, a function which still takes place annually. Geoffrey was a regular attender and obviously greatly enjoyed these reunions. Invariably he and I sat together and we always had most enjoyable and fascinating talk, ranging from mutual war-time memories, life at Cambridge and Ely, and even, as I well remember on one occasion, a philosophical discussion on the authenticity of the Turin shroud.

It was only after the war that any of us realised what a distinguished scholar he was. He was never one to sing his own praises or achievements. We had only known him as a good and brave man.

In the last few years it was obvious that he was very sick, but he never referred to his illness and nor did we, and this I am sure was how he wanted it to be.

London Gazette 1944

MILITARY CROSS

Chaplain IV Class Geoffrey William Hugo LAMPE
(RAChdD)
HQ 34 Tank Brigade

Rev. G. W. H. LAMPE, RAChdD, has been in action with 147 Regt. RAC continuously and is still in action with this Regt. Throughout he has been in and amongst the forward troops under shell and mortar fire. His presence there and his complete disregard of personal safety has done much to maintain the high standard and morale in this Regt.

On a great many occasions he has assisted in recovering the bodies of fatal casualties from destroyed and burnt-out tanks and has conducted burials under shell and mortar fire. These actions have further heightened the morale of the troops.

No praise is high enough for the conduct of this Chaplain in and amongst the forward troops, and without doubt his presence and personal example have been of the greatest value and of a very high order.

His gallantry and devotion to duty have been an inspiration to all.

by The Reverend Canon F. Bussby, MBE, MA

The late Canon Bussby was a Chaplain to the Forces and
played a leading part in selecting and training Ordinands
from the Forces in the Middle East and in Germany where he
was Staff Chaplain, HQ, 21 Army Group, 1944–5. He had a
varied pastoral experience—as an Oxford College Chaplain,
as Vice-Principal of a Theological College, and as a Parish
Priest. Latterly, he was a Canon Residentiary of Winchester
Cathedral—Canon Treasurer for three years, then Canon
Librarian. He was also Vice-Dean. He died suddenly in 1981,
while leading a party in the Holy Land, and leaves a widow.

During our undergraduate days, when Mussolini and Hitler were
coming into the news, I came to have a passing knowledge of
Geoffrey Lampe. He was clearly a man of great ability. Equally
clearly he was a modest man. His brilliant record was not
surprising.

In 1937 our ways parted. He went to his curacy in Devon: I to my
curacy near Liverpool. Being three years older than Geoffrey I was
able to be accepted as a chaplain in the Army on the Regular Army
Reserve of Officers in May 1939 and so found myself mobilised
before the Second World War was declared. As soon as it was
possible for him, Geoffrey received an Emergency Commission in
the Army and was embodied in 1941. During these years our paths
were still separate. My service had taken me to the BEF and to the
MEF and had baptised me with fire in the invasion of Crete in
1941. Geoffrey's service, after a period at home, led him to
Normandy with the 34th Tank Brigade. At this time I was junior
Staff Chaplain to the HQ of 21 Army Group, of which the 34th
Tank Brigade was a part. Our postings brought us together again
after seven years. Our first task was the winning of the war and here
Geoffrey played, as might be expected, a quiet but very significant
part. His brigade saw much of the heavy fighting and his courage
during the campaign gave him (the first chaplain in Normandy to
be so gazetted) the MC.

Geoffrey and others were aware that the important issue in
winning the war was to prepare for peace. Here thoughts were
concentrated upon the Church and her ministry. No man, unless
unfit for military service, had been able to begin training for the
ministry since the outbreak of war. The encouragement of
candidates for the ministry was therefore a most important part of

the chaplains' work. Shortly after 'D' Day 1944 the chaplains had set aside one of their number to prepare precisely for this situation. He immediately set about discovering who had such thoughts about his life in the post-war world. In due course he discovered about four hundred men with this particular thought. The discovery indicated that a great task lay ahead and that help was urgently needed both from the Church at home and, more immediately, from the chaplains in the field. Here Geoffrey was outstandingly an obvious person to give that help. No soldier or service man who knew the realities of war could accuse him of being unaware of what he had undergone. In addition Geoffrey still carried with him his enormous powers of mind and spirit. We were fortunate to have such a man on active service. He brought, to an outstanding degree, the very qualities which we needed. And so renewed acquaintance soon became a close fellowship in this special field of assisting and selecting men for the ministry of the Church.

Early in 1945 therefore I had the task of preparing for the first selection conference for ordinands. Such a conference had both to satisfy the Church at home and to meet the contingencies of the services. The preparation therefore had to be made both in England and in Brussels. The Church had appointed Leslie Owen as Bishop of Maidstone to be Bishop to the Forces. He was our link. In the end he was both convinced and helpful, coming over to Brussels for the very first conference which was planned for 3–7 May in 1945. This meant knowing the way the services work. Candidates had no special leave and had to arrange their leave allocation (such as is given to all service men) to attend the conference. All these technicalities were overcome and candidates and selectors (the Bishop, three chaplains, and one officer) undertook the first selection conference on the continent of Europe. In retrospect we can congratulate those concerned on the timing of the conference. The results of the conference were known on VE Day, 8 May 1945. It could not be said that the Church had been hesitant or wavering when decision was required. The part played by Geoffrey did much to assure the authorities at home that we were not unqualified to undertake the task. Geoffrey shared the lecturing in this and several conferences held in the summer of 1945 at the Church Houses in Brussels and Antwerp and in the Church Houses belonging to each of the three Corps in Germany. Geoffrey also was one of the selectors assessing men as to their suitability for Orders. Again, his judgement was immensely valuable. In that first conference he shared the lectures with the Bishop of Maidstone.

In the summer of 1945 men began to come home after six years in the armed services and we tried to 'select' men whose turn for demobilisation came first. In addition we gave them, where possible (parallel to the facilities afforded to service men who wished to return to one of many different walks in life) a month of pre-training, this time in theology so that they could undertake university or theological college work without too much strain after being away from their books, in some cases for twice the length of a university degree.

Working with Geoffrey to provide such facilities within a sympathetic framework (due not a little to Field Marshal Montgomery) was one of life's most rewarding and exciting experiences. The war-time links continued for a time. During his Easter vacations in 1946 and 1947 he joined me at Lichfield where the Central Advisory Council of Training for the Ministry had established a special Selection Centre for those being demobilised. His rich gifts of mind and spirit which had been tested in the harsh realities of war, made him a colleague in this work of inestimable value.

by the Reverend Canon A. Inglis, MA

Canon Inglis, now in retirement in Lincolnshire, is an Honorary Canon of Southwell, to which diocese he has devoted much of his ministry as an incumbent, a University Chaplain, and a teacher. He ministered as a Chaplain to the Forces throughout the war, and was mentioned in dispatches. Like the late Canon Bussby, he played a part, with Geoffrey Lampe, in selecting and training Ordination Candidates from the Forces in Germany.

The first meeting with Geoffrey was immediately after the Reichwald battle. It was intensely cold, the area most desolate and in every way unpleasant. He was at the moment of my arrival out and about; but I was 'taken charge of' by his batman driver, a delightfully 'rough egg' of a man whose general demeanour failed to suggest much concern with military discipline. He was of course entirely devoted to Geoffrey with a single-minded concern both for his comfort and safety. In due time, Geoffrey appeared, coming into view with the same characteristic stride (plus pipe) which always made the day go better when encountered at the turn of a corner in Cambridge or elsewhere in later years. He was tired, but full of the cheerful comment so unfailingly apt, gentle and wonderfully phrased. My concern had been to deliver a message about promotion and the reason for it from Willie Tindal who was Staff Chaplain at HQ. It was (probably rightly) suspected that neither of us would welcome removal from the front line assignments. The fighting was almost over. Tindal was anxious about ordinands and other matters which he had been concerned to strengthen. He was about to return to Edinburgh to teach in New College. Many later problems would not have appeared had he been available. However, we were immediately posted to what appeared to be non-existent jobs, but which issued in my taking over the work of the Central Advisory Council of Training for the Ministry (CACTM) in succession to Fred Bussby, and Geoffrey's taking care of an Area Church House.

As regards collecting together the men who were offering themselves for ordination, it was a case of working against time because, rather unwisely, I had agreed to defer demobilisation for six months. There were lists to be prepared and releases to be secured which meant much detailed work and the beginnings of the now accepted selection conference procedures. Fortunately

Geoffrey's relationship with Eric Treacy and Philip Wheeldon was firmly based in mutual regard and co-operation. Previously, I had been attached to Yorkshire troops fighting alongside the Canadian Army and was very much out of that particular 'swim'. But in due time the papers and so on were brought up from Brussels to Herford the HQ. Three Church Houses, one for each of the British areas, were established. Geoffrey had taken over a shooting lodge belonging to the von Kramm family in lovely country at Verden near Celle. Besides recurring CACTM selection conferences there were a series of three-day occasions with all sorts of people . . . it was a kind of extended Padre's Hour discussion with a background of quiet and worship. Of course Geoffrey excelled in all this . . . very much 'mine host' to all comers and yet immediately deeply loved and respected. A marvellous 'classlessness' put both generals and the toughest of Glaswegians at ease. Once it was established that wine at the evening meal was appropriate only on Sundays and Thursdays, quiet and good order came spontaneously. Not far away from the stillness and remoteness of the hills and woods, in which Geoffrey loved to discover fresh walks, there was the beat of the main road of the area which was an escape route for gypsies and other groups avoiding the advance of the Russians. . . . On one memorable day the Duke of Brunswick appeared with a succession of farm carts containing art treasures and other valuables from his nearby castle which was about to be absorbed into the Russian Zone.

One of the problems had been that some of the Regular Army Chaplains had displayed no small hostility to the CACTM, and, by extension, to the Church House, projects. After much discussion it transpired that they objected to 'mixed' gatherings, in that officers and other ranks shared both the same selection conferences and the retreats. It had not occurred to us that rank in the narrow sense should not as far as possible be disregarded. But it did mean that Geoffrey and the house at Preetz in Schleswig-Holstein (with Philip Wheeldon, Patrick Ashton, Mark Green, and David Galliford in charge) became essential to the whole enterprise. Unfortunately Geoffrey, with his direct responsibility in Hanover, could not appear much in Preetz. This became the centre for two or three pre-vocational courses which aimed at abstracting men from an army situation before demobilisation and providing a month's quite exacting academic training, with some time for relaxation and thought within a unique and unforgettable setting. Pat Ashton who became Rector of Sandringham made the place a delight to visit . . . Geoffrey's advice and encouragement were always invaluable. He was able to cut out all sorts of non-essentials and fasten upon basic simplicities. I remember his skilful summaries of Biblical books and key passages. Even then he seemed to have read, remembered, and thought about everything. Sometimes his judgements of candidates seemed unjustifiably kindly, but usually they proved to be correct in that he disregarded the more negative side of things. But he could administer with a glance the sort of rebuke which encouraged no second offence.

One curious incident. Part of the smooth operation of the work depended upon Vivian Symons, one of the first six staff officers chosen by Field Marshal Montgomery to plan 'D' Day. He had become an ordinand. It stirred in my head that there was something in the Oxford Statutes about a Staff College distinction excusing the Smalls entrance exam. This proved to be the case and with Geoffrey's help Symons was enrolled at Wycliffe Hall and took a degree in theology. He repaid Geoffrey in a curious way. Geoffrey had been elected into a Fellowship at St John's and there was anxiety to have him installed before the end of the summer term. This was duly arranged and the papers were in order but the weeks passed and nothing happened. Towards the end of September Symons was asked to check the progress, which he did. This made it possible to discover that the papers had for some weeks been reposing in the IN tray of a Royal Army Chaplains' Department official. Geoffrey was therefore able to be in Oxford for the Michaelmas term. Vivian Symons was devoted to Geoffrey who helped him in a variety of ways. It was remarkable that Geoffrey could always engage with the people with whom he had to do at their level and pace. No doubt it was part of his selflessness. There was never any pretence and, because he worked from within himself, no need to 'adjust' in any snobbish way to his environment or company. There was the same authenticity about his demeanour when he turned the corner in the snow near Nijmegen as at the Oxford garden parties and other occasions in which he always so readily and characteristically delighted. No doubt others will have memories of him in the various post-war commitments in which there was so much personal fulfilment and enrichment of others.

One of the problems which Geoffrey was able to solve with Philip Wheeldon was the need for other denominations to have speedy and direct access to their ordinands. In fact there were not very many; but various highly-placed people arrived. It was important to keep the Church of England conferences going to time and also to overcome the incredible 'block' in Church House, Westminster, which tended to cause men on leave, longing to get home, to be tied up in London, waiting to be 'processed'. The process was by no means speedy nor accessible. No doubt there were difficulties. It was the usual form to send the visiting dignitaries to Geoffrey who somehow occupied them cheerfully and reassuringly. It brought what could have been, especially with the Methodists, a rather brittle situation much more within control. It was an example of his capacity to put lesser problems into a wider and more positive setting. There was one amusing story of a distinguished visitor which Geoffrey loved to retail. Some bright sparks had wanted (for one and the only time) to witness a boar hunt. The estate retainers were overjoyed to oblige and it was all set up. No one realised the unsporting barbarity of the procedure, i.e. to drive the boar through a thicket across a ten-foot drive, whilst on the other side anything up to half a dozen guns were in position to shoot the animal as it broke cover. But there was almost disaster in that a visiting dignitary of overlarge proportions, apparently a genial and cheerful character, had taken himself for a walk, and instead of confronting a wild boar the shooting party were brought face to face with a smiling and most interested visitor . . . Happily, Geoffrey's persistent and sincere desire to further ecumenical relations more than survived this and various other shocks.

4

ST JOHN'S COLLEGE, OXFORD

by the Right Reverend K. J. Woollcombe, MA

Bishop Woollcombe was a pupil of Geoffrey Lampe at St
John's College, Oxford, and succeeded him there as Chaplain
and Fellow, and, like Geoffrey Lampe, was subsequently
elected into an Honorary Fellowship. He has been a Professor
at General Theological Seminary, New York, and Principal
of Edinburgh Theological College. From 1971 to 1978 he was
Bishop of Oxford. Since then, he has been an Assistant
Bishop in the Diocese of London, and is now a Canon of St
Paul's.

I was one of the second 'wave' of ex-servicemen who went up to St
John's College, Oxford for the first time in October 1946. Geoffrey
had been demobilised a year earlier and had already collected a
number of pupils, most of whom, like Hugh Montefiore (now
Bishop of Birmingham), had matriculated before the war and
needed only a relatively short time to complete their degree courses.
My year consisted of older men whose war service had prevented
them from matriculating earlier, younger men straight from school,
and men who had chosen to spend a few terms at the college during
the war before being called up. We were therefore a disparate
group, both in age and experience, and had to spend two or three
years as undergraduates. This in itself posed a major problem to us
and to our tutors: *status pupillaris* was not an easy role for those
who had been in command of ships, aircraft, or battalions. But that
was not our only difficulty: most of us had forgotten how to write
English after years of service jargon; some of us had lost our
original vocation, others had just discovered one, and others, like
myself, simply did not know what kind of post-war career to

choose. I had been awarded an open exhibition in Classics in 1941 but had subsequently been trained as a naval engineer; I knew that I did not have the aptitude for Greats and decided to read Engineering. Almost at once I began to realise that I had made a serious mistake because I was incapable of understanding the mathematics and physics which were a necessary preliminary to the Honour School of Engineering. At the same time I was undergoing a crisis of faith: brought up a rigorous High Churchman, I had experienced increasing difficulty in reconciling the religion which I practised with what I actually believed. I was also in love and impatient to get married!

It was at this stage that I plucked up the courage to knock at the door where so many of my friends had found help, just inside the front quad on the left. Geoffrey knew a great deal about vocation; although not much more than a decade older than ourselves, he had been a curate, a schoolmaster, a soldier, and a don. As an army chaplain he had given invaluable counsel to service ordination candidates in Germany. The secret of his success as a counsellor lay in his ability to listen and to remember what he had heard, even though the jumbled story might have lasted a long time. His manner was gentle and entirely non-directive: 'You might like to consider . . .' or 'I rather think that . . .' were the phrases which came most naturally to him. He won immediate trust by the warmth of his friendship and by the serious concern which showed in his eyes—marvellous eyes which could radiate love, laughter, and compassion all at once.

No sooner had I told it than my problem was solved. 'Why don't you try Theology?' he asked; 'It's an interesting subject and you could manage the languages.' I protested that I was not at all sure that I should offer myself for ordination, but he countered the objection quickly with the observation that as I *was* sure that I could not continue in Engineering, I might do a lot worse than read a subject which would help me to sort out my religious difficulties and prepare me for almost any career. So the greatest and happiest decision of my life was made and a friendship, equal to none in strength, began.

Geoffrey's skill as a teacher lay in his capacity to wait patiently for his pupils to be gripped by, and to grasp their subject. He never criticised until he was sure that we had the confidence to respond to his criticism, and even then it would more often than not be in fun.

In a note to me, dated Whitsunday 1948, he wrote, 'A small point that occurred to me after your last essay was that it read as though Leo XIII was responsible for 1870, thus depriving Pio Nono of the triumphant conclusion of his quite disastrous life's work. I don't suppose you intended any such thing, but it sounded rather like it'.

My first task was to read the Bible over and over again until I knew what I was writing about. My essays were dreadfully thin and rather stilted; I do not suppose they took more than a quarter of an hour to read. But they gave Geoffrey the opportunity to teach me how to use commentaries and dictionaries and where to find them. Books were hard to get, and Blackwell's entire stock of theology filled only a few shelves in the front of the (then) cramped shop in the Broad. We depended greatly on libraries and on sharing the books that could be obtained. At first it all seemed dull and heavy going; marking the Pentateuch with coloured pencils to distinguish J from E and P was not much fun and seemed to obscure what the text actually contained. But real theology sprang to life with Amos: here was a prophet who spoke clearly to our condition in the early years of the making of the welfare state, a man after my own heart with a passion for social justice and fire in his belly. It was Amos who convinced me that I was at last on course and who inspired me to find a way to reconcile the theory and practice of the Christian faith. But it was Geoffrey who opened my eyes to what Amos had to say in the twentieth century and let me see it for myself.

In those days a college tutor in theology took his men through the whole gamut of the subject, unless they elected to specialise in a particularly obscure branch of it. The system had its advantages as well as drawbacks; although Geoffrey was an amateur in Old Testament studies, he knew the text so well that he had a great deal of it by heart and was more familiar than most with its background. He had been elected into his fellowship during the war and had made friends in the SCR with Claude Schaeffer, the archaeologist of Ras Shamra-Ugarit, who combined his duties as an officer in the Free French Navy with a Senior Research Fellowship in the college. We were introduced to Claude in the easy and natural way in which Geoffrey brought all his friends together, and I remember being fascinated by Claude's plain man's guide to the significance of Ras Shamra, shared with anybody who cared to sit in Geoffrey's room one Monday evening after Hall.

The success of this particular talk enables me to write about the homogeneity of Geoffrey's ministry as tutor and chaplain. The three *foci* of his ministry to his pupils were the weekly tutorial (always given individually at great personal cost in time and energy), the weekly class on Saturday mornings on the set texts, for all his pupils at St John's and St Peter's Hall, and the Monday evening discussions open to everyone. All other members of the College had likewise three regular opportunities to meet the chaplain: in addition to the Monday discussions there were the Sunday evening sermons (two from the chaplain and two from visiting preachers in each term) and Dean's Prayers at 8.0 a.m. or Compline at 10.15 p.m. every day. To read theology was not to be enclosed in a kind of holy club but rather to be admitted to membership of a family which extended in different ways and included all kinds of people, not all of whom were churchmen or Christians. The fact that we were often welcomed to the house in Museum Road (and sometimes invited to baby-sit!) gave us a strong sense of loyalty to Geoffrey as our paterfamilias.

He was also our father in God, not in a paternalist way, but in the sense that like any good father (and he was a very good father) he shared freely with us his own understanding of a subject and helped us to form a view of our own. Alec Graham (now Bishop of Newcastle) who read Modern Languages describes his technique admirably.

'I went up to St John's as a text-book Anglo-Catholic: he never sought to dissuade me, for he was large enough to respect any point of view which was securely based and well argued. But over four years his massive erudition and his ability to turn a subject inside out had its effect on me, making me as much liberal as catholic. His sermons were a trifle ponderous, but over thirty years later I can remember how he treated some subjects. For instance, he started with the expression "the mystical body of Chirst" as applied to the Church and concluded that this expression was better used with reference to the Eucharist, while the term "the body of Christ" was more suitably applied to the Church than to the Eucharist. His Monday evening groups in his rooms were especially influential on me: there I learned from his example and with his encouragement to formulate my own views, to express them with precision and to explore the Christian world. His own technique I noticed then and frequently afterwards (for instance, when he came to Worcester to talk to undergraduates and to Lincoln to address theological students): he would set out with great thoroughness the basis of his subject; then he would venture out with quite a number of (to me) new ideas and imaginative possibilities; if tackled, he would retreat if necessary to a prepared position, from which he could not be dislodged, for he had set out his basis with such care and reasonableness that it could not be shaken.'

He adopted the same technique with his pupils, encouraging the abler men to pursue adventurous theories, but content to let all go at their own pace, provided that they were prepared to work. People who did not work bored him. My own speculations were occasionally outrageous: in expounding Acts 21.18–36, I ventured the hypothesis that James, in sending Paul to the Temple, was knowingly and deliberately putting him in the way of certain arrest and deportation to Rome in order to get rid of an awkward theologian. Geoffrey's laughter, which I suppose could be heard all over the quad, was enough to make me forget it very quickly. But nearly twenty years later he recalled it, to my intense embarrassment, at a meeting of a learned society.

If laughter spiced his tutorials, as it often did, his pugnacity gave them zest. 1946 had seen the publication of *The Apostolic Ministry*, edited by Kenneth Kirk, then Bishop of Oxford. The crucial New Testament essay in the collection had been contributed by the late Dom Gregory Dix, OSB, of whose scholarship Geoffrey was suspicious. (Later he was to write to me, 'Whenever I have listened to the persuasive voice of the late Dom Gregory I have fallen into some kind of snare'.) A number of my essays in 1947 developed into arguments about Dom Gregory's theory of the apostolate because I was by nature and upbringing disposed to accept it, whereas Geoffrey's liberal and evangelical stance kept him in the opposite camp. He was then writing his Albrecht Stumpff Memorial Lecture, *Some Aspects of the New Testament Ministry*, and I think he was glad to have me as a sparring partner. We certainly enjoyed our debates which had a profoundly formative influence upon my own view of the emergence of the episcopate. When I wrote to congratulate him on the lecture, he replied, 'It is not a weighty contribution; it is designed (a) to call attention to some of the continental work on the question, most of which approaches it from the linguistic side instead of from either modern Anglicanism or modern Nonconformity; (b) to have a crack at Kirk and his boys'.

In the first of his two objects he was entirely successful, though it cost him a good many barrels of midnight oil to improve his German. 'I wish it were not such labour to read these German works,' he wrote. 'You should learn that tongue as soon as you can, and make a better job of it than I did.' In the second he was also successful, but I am inclined to think that he needed the stimulus of a keen debate to bring out his best work; we should never have had *The Seal of the Spirit* if he had not been eager for a second round with Dom Gregory. Nevertheless I have always felt that it was a little quixotic to choose to tilt at the Trinity in his Bamptons, even though they make me feel glad to be an Anglican with the freedom to question the most fundamental doctrine of all. Or is it? The argument of *God as Spirit* is cogent and has yet to be answered adequately.

Geoffrey's concern for his pupils did not come to an end with the delicious dinner he gave them after Schools—as a rule playing joint-host with his friend Blair Leishman to those who had been reading Theology or English Literature. There were congratulations for success, however modest: to one who had made the third class he said, 'You seemed to have spent such an elegant summer term that I did have some misgivings. And when you told me after the last paper that all was well, then I was really alarmed'. There was deep commiseration for the disappointed, which in my own case meant giving me a paid job on the *Lexicon of Patristic Greek* and encouraging me to enter for a University Prize. He knew that I needed hard work and a fresh goal, as well as the warmth of his friendship and pastoral care.

Like most tutors of his generation he preferred to maintain a rather formal relationship with his pupils until they graduated. After graduation the formality vanished and we felt more relaxed in his company; he continued to take a keen interest in us long after we had gone down and there would always be prayers and greetings for ordination, marriage, and the birth of our children. To anyone who wanted to do post-graduate work he showed particular kindness, and would spend hours helping to get the field of research correctly described and delineated for consideration by the Board of the Faculty. I found his guidance at this stage invaluable: it is not easy for a beginner to find his way about the texts of the Greek and Latin Fathers, and he was exceedingly generous with advice and help. He would also keep an eye on our careers, never failing to draw our attention to academic or ecclesiastical posts for which he thought we should apply.

I doubt whether in those days he took enough time off; he had a heavy teaching load and was spending hours of what ought to have been his leisure on the Patristic Lexicon in addition to writing *The Seal of the Spirit*. But there were family picnics in Bagley Wood and the *walks*. Hugh Montefiore writes, 'I still remember with dread his summons, "Come out for a walk with me next week," and his short cuts over ploughed fields'. David Jowitt (now Canon of St Mary's Cathedral, Edinburgh) recalls Blair Leishman in khaki shorts, shirt, and a rucksack striding along beside Geoffrey in clerical suit and a collar, both puffing their pipes, as they toured the villages of Oxfordshire. And there were holidays in the gipsy caravan, choir outings to college livings, for cricket in the summer and carols in the winter. His pleasures were as traditional and as simple as his clothes, and he was not given to luxuries, except on one occasion. He decided to buy a car and sought my advice before going to the Motor Show to choose one. We agreed that a relatively simple family vehicle would be the best buy. He returned with a huge white Vauxhall and blushed as he introduced me to it, 'You see, Elizabeth liked the colour'.

In correspondence with my fellow-pupils the words 'large', 'massive', and 'Olympian' have been frequent descriptions of his nature and ability. If he sometimes found it difficult to communicate with us, he never evinced a trace of impatience. We knew that our tutor was a large-hearted man, generous in mind and spirit, and we were glad and proud to have been taught by him. Though we may have had ten thousand other tutors in Christ, we had but one father to whom we were devoted.

5

THE YEARS AT BIRMINGHAM, 1953–60

by Professor the Reverend Canon J. G. Davies, DD

Professor Davies, who is a DD of Oxford, has, after a curacy in Rotherhithe, exercised a mainly academic ministry. He succeeded Geoffrey Lampe in the Edward Cadbury Chair at Birmingham, and is the author of many works on early church history. He is an Honorary Canon of Birmingham.

Geoffrey was elected to the Edward Cadbury Chair of Theology in the University of Birmingham in the summer of 1952, but he did not assume his duties until the following year, spending the intervening months winding up the Patristic Lexicon office in Oxford.

The department, of which he was the third head—being preceded by H. G. Wood and H. F. D. Sparks and hence the initial prevalence of humorous remarks about wood, sparks, and lamp—was at that time a small one by any reckoning. There was only one other full time member of staff, although assistance was available from ten Recognized Lecturers, who were scholars working in the Midlands and approved by the university. The total of students in all categories—Single Honours, Combined Honours, Diploma, etc.—was only fifteen.

It can be said without fear of contradiction that Geoffrey's major contribution to the development of the department lay not in innovation but in consolidation. Some slight modifications were introduced into the first year of the BA syllabus, but the majority of courses remained unchanged with Geoffrey spending most time on

New Testament teaching and Systematics. Staff and students however steadily increased under his leadership. In 1956 he was successful in arranging for the establishment of a second lectureship (in the Old Testament) and in his final year at Birmingham he had managed to persuade the faculty to make provision for another in Church History and he had begun negotiations with a charitable trust to fund a second chair to be devoted to the area of overlap between theology, the natural sciences, and philosophy. The annual number of students, by the time of his departure, had risen to forty-eight.

Geoffrey soon made an impression in university circles, so much so that within the short span of two years he had been elected dean of the faculty of arts. A verse from this period, communicated by Emeritus Professor Harry Cronne (formerly of Medieval History), reveals in what affectionate regard he was held by his colleagues.

> A genial priest you see in me,
> L-mp-, learned in Theology.
> The light I shed shall grow still brighter—
> Unless extinguished by a mitre.

Deans in the 1950s were a different breed from those required in the post-Robbins' era. The faculty in those days was hardly a third of its present size and admitted only two hundred students each year. This meant that the nature and extent of the dean's work was entirely different from what it was to become in the succeeding decade. Geoffrey's calm confidence and quite evident benevolence kept him undisturbed in office; he could and did sit lightly to administrative duties and yet accomplished with ease most of what was required. Mr Clifford Brackwell, who was assistant registrar at the time and therefore best able to observe him in his decanal role, reminisces as follows:

> As dean Professor Lampe was able to keep a low profile, as we say—so low as to be almost out of sight of most of the faculty most of the time. I dare say there were times when this was exasperating, but in those days it was not altogether intolerable if a dean disappeared without trace for extended periods—perhaps caravanning in Wales—and left the faculty to run itself for a bit: the faculty could afford to have a non-interventionist *laissez-faire* dean and I do not think we came to any harm. The university was only just beginning to impose

the sort of central control and direction that we have come to accept. It was indeed in such a context as this that I only ever saw Professor Lampe angry. It was when the senate, for the first time, laid down faculty admissions figures. He had no doubt been there when it was done, but he had not taken the point that this set a faculty admissions *maximum* and he was so incensed that we should not ourselves decide how many students we could teach that he immediately rang the registrar and protested with quite unusual vehemence for him. On that occasion he was very jealous of the faculty's autonomy. This episode however was rather uncharacteristic. In general Professor Lampe was disposed to be as conciliatory as possible—almost to a fault. His inclination was to smooth things over rather than risk a clash. As a chairman he was prone to pass on to the next item of business before a clear decision had been reached. With that qualification he was a good chairman. He did not much like having to attend meetings, and if he had to he liked them to be short. He did not do much homework but he was very quick on the uptake and unsurpassed at extemporising. He played things largely by ear and his ear was sensitive and responsive.

What did the faculty think of him as a dean? No one would say he was untiringly industrious or zealous, or that he gave a strong lead. But then deans were not supposed to be like that in those days. I am sure the faculty found his rule benign and reasonable. He had no particular axe to grind and he used his authority with impartiality. For my part I found him very good to work with as a person—kind, co-operative, level-headed, unpretentious and unfussy.

Indeed there never was any danger that Geoffrey would change his birthright of scholarship for a pottage of bureaucracy. His industry really showed itself in the many addresses he gave up and down the country and abroad and in the articles and books he published, while all the time working on the Lexicon.

Some of his public lectures were very carefully prepared, such as his Maurice Lectures at King's College, London, of 1955, published the following year with the title *Reconciliation in Christ*—this is an investigation of the relationship between justification and theories of the atonement. At other times his undoubted gift of extemporisation was much to the fore. He was heard to remark on one occasion that he always had to listen carefully when a chairman introduced him in order to discover the topic on which he was billed to speak. Needless to say, when he did stand up, his delivery was fluent and faultless, the content invariably interesting, frequently profound and no one could have suspected from his magisterial performance that this was not the fruit of much writing and rewriting. In this connection a thumbnail sketch provided by Mr Brackwell is very apt and by no means untypical:

> I am sitting one evening in the Edmund Street SCR. Also there are G.W.H.L. and an eager young clergyman. It is clear that the latter has written something and sent it to Lampe for comment. It is equally clear that Lampe has not yet read it, but he improvises so brilliantly that the young man, who is doing most of the talking, never suspects this. A masterly performance!

It was in his after dinner speeches that Geoffrey's sense of humour and of fun revealed itself most felicitously. There was the occasion of a senate dinner, given by Robert (now Sir Robert) Aitken, the vice-chancellor, when Geoffrey began by recalling a Marx Brothers film and quoting Groucho as thanking his hostess in these words: 'We've had a wonderful time, but this was not it'. To the delight of all present, who had initially reacted with a loud gasp, this was quickly translated into an elegant compliment.

Mischievous at times, he had a subterranean *joie de vivre* that bubbled to the surface every now and again, as when he and Elizabeth took friends to dinner dances in remote Black Country hostelries or entertained in their large house on the Bristol Road, not excluding the annual 'Punch before Lunch' on Boxing Days and their numerous parties.

This sociability was also combined with intellectual fare, as when he acted as the regular host to a 'Religious Study Circle'. Composed of theologians and philosophers, with an infusion of local incumbents, this met once a month to hear a paper and discuss over a cup of tea and a cake. This mention of the clergy may serve to call attention to the fact that Geoffrey was not only a university man but also a churchman, as was recognized in 1957 when he was made an honorary canon of Birmingham cathedral. Not that all his pronouncements found favour with every cleric, especially as he was never reticent in espousing unpopular causes if he felt them to be right. He was a firm proponent of intercommunion, long before the practice had become widespread. More especially, when Womens' Lib. was not yet on the distant horizon, he advocated the ordination of women with well supported arguments that were difficult to counter.

His balanced approach to doctrinal topics made him a formidable opponent—here was no enthusiast mouthing unsubstantial prejudices, but a scholar who used his learning with ease and therefore all the more effectively. One has only to read *I Believe*—published in 1960, just before he moved to Ely and therefore a fruit of his Birmingham years—to perceive his quiet mastery of those subjects upon which he chose to concentrate. *I Believe* is of course a statement of personal faith, but, as he himself noted in the foreword, it was 'written from the standpoint of one whose understanding of Christianity is determined in the main by the Historic Creeds and the Anglican Prayer Book'. It is a summary account of the central and fundamental doctrines of the Church and, while it does not shed new light upon them, it certainly brings out their meaning with the utmost clarity. Firmly rooted in a critical approach to the Bible, with a sympathetic understanding of the continuous experience of the Church and not insensitive to modern questions, this remains, even after twenty years, an admirably lucid exposition of the traditional teaching embodied in the Apostles' Creed.

He was however never narrowly partisan but manifested the spirit of true ecumenism by seeking the truth amid all extremes. This is very evident in his contribution to *The Doctrine of Justification by Faith* (1954) which he also edited. His purpose was to examine the supposed opposition between the Protestant *sola fide* and the Catholic emphasis upon the sacraments. Confining himself deliberately in the main to the New Testament, he presented a closely argued case that fully supported his conclusion:

> It is, then, clear enough that 'faith alone' means 'faith without works of merit'. It does not mean faith without sacraments, nor a subjective and individualistic adherence to Christ which ignores the Church . . . What the tradition which we may call Protestant does fear is rather, an inadequate, because impersonal, theology of grace in sacramental doctrine. The

sacraments are effectual signs of the personal operation of the living Lord. They are not to be regarded and valued as though they were 'things'; they are modes of Christ's encounter with us. I must therefore admit to some embarrassment when I hear the old and very common expression, 'to use the sacraments'. This is a very small point; but such language seems to me to savour of that sub-personal conception of the sacraments and sacramental grace from which I believe the implications of the doctrine of justification by faith alone, when it is properly understood, should help to preserve our thinking.

This passage has been quoted at length because it illustrates perfectly Geoffrey's consistent and judicious application of the Anglican triple basis—Bible, tradition and the use of sound reason.

He was much in demand for conferences and commissions, either of the Church of England or of the World Council of Churches. Amongst other functions, he served as vice-chairman of the European section of the Faith and Order Theology Commission on Christ and the Church and in this capacity made his contribution to numerous reports, such as *One Lord One Baptism* (1960). This last was indeed published in a series called 'Studies in Ministry and Worship' which he had been editing with David M. Paton of the SCM Press. As regards engagements outside the confines of the university, Geoffrey was a person who found it almost impossible to say 'no' to any invitation. This meant that from time to time he would discover—usually at the last minute—that he was supposed to be in two places at once, addressing a conference in Derby and recording a Third Programme Broadcast in London, or giving a lecture in Cambridge to some society or other while being required in Geneva for a consultation. This did not unduly worry him and those who were gently invited to deputise usually found the experience worthwhile.

To equip himself the better for these peregrinations, he took driving lessons during visits to Oxford, arranged between strings of other engagements. The car he eventually acquired was large and powerful and was apparently the sole medium through which he ever expressed real aggression. To be his passenger from Birmingham to some other centre was to have a comparatively peaceful journey as far as the derestriction sign at the edge of the conurbation, at which point Geoffrey took off, not unlike an aeroplane about to leave a runway—the car shuddered, the speed shot up, the countryside flew by, one's eyeballs were pressed a little towards the back of one's skull. Nevertheless, no casualties ensued!

As a colleague, within the department of theology, he was very easy to work with. His affability and ease of manner produced a relaxed atmosphere and he was always concerned to promote the academic interest of those junior to himself. In term he was no absentee professor and despite an overfull programme of papers to read, lectures to give, etc., outside Birmingham, he took his full share in teaching, post-graduate supervision, and administration. He tended to work in the mornings in his office in Great Charles Street, in the centre of the city at the rear of the old Mason College building, where in the 1950s the faculty of arts, unlike the rest of the university at the Edgbaston site, was still housed. His room being next to a well patronised public house, with walls of white tiles, relics of a chemistry lab but suggesting a convenience, he was liable to be interrupted by slightly inebriated gentlemen who seemed always ready to engage in theological discussion of a kind. So there was the tall figure who once stumbled over the threshold, pointed a solemn finger at him and asked: 'Who are you?' Upon being told he was speaking to the professor of theology, he demanded: 'What happened in the year 4004 BC?' This particular office, which has long since vanished beneath the new city reference library, had a plethora of tiny built-in cupboards. Sheets and sheets of hand-written notes about the theological and ecclesiastical vocabulary of the Greek Christian authors were piled within them. In one there was an aged gas meter, crushed against which were to be seen at one time a dust-covered heap of files relating to university committees that the previous dean had fondly handed over to Geoffrey when he assumed that office—they cluttered the space, but their contents were obviously never allowed to clutter his mind.

As one who had undergone training for the ministry at Queen's (Theological) College, he was pleased to become a member of its council, contributing wise advice in the course of its deliberations. He sought to stimulate the ordinands, promote the interests of the college in all ways possible and bring it into closer and closer association with the department. It is on record that he was also a member of the university's masonic lodge, although knowledge of his activities in that sphere is inevitably limited.

Geoffrey received the final accolade of the university in 1957 when he became its vice-principal. To the surprise of some, he did not relinquish the deanship, which had one more year to run, but continued to shoulder the responsibilities jointly, and then the vice-principalship alone for the remaining two sessions in Birmingham. His nomination to the post by the vice-chancellor was influenced by three factors: first, the need to preserve at the centre of the administration a balance between representatives of the science and arts based subjects; second, his undoubted willingness to serve wherever he was wanted, and, third, the recognition of his charm and ease of manner as a public figure and therefore of his eminent suitability to act as an ambassador of the university to the world outside. He was not, at this juncture at least, a person to steer complex business through countless meetings and committees. Indeed, his indifference to prolonged discussion of the minutiae of administration, together with his imperturbability, were strikingly illustrated by his conduct of business at the first meeting of senate that he had to chair in the absence of the vice-chancellor. Easter was very late that year, and the registrar had proposed a re-organisation of the dates of the summer term so that it could begin before the festival; this was linked with a further proposal that the technical and secretarial staff should take a break at some other time. Geoffrey's contribution was a prolonged chuckle coupled with the observation that not even the senate of the university of Birmingham could override the Council of Nicea. The uproar was immediate. Geoffrey simply hove to and let the storm blow over, as it did very quickly.

As a man with an undoubted presence, which was not simply an effect of his tall stature, he won good opinions for the university he represented on whatever occasions he appeared. But it was probably the conferring on him of the honorary degree of Doctor of Divinity by the university of Edinburgh in 1959 that gave him the greatest pleasure at this time and in a sense foreshadowed the imminent appearance of the first fascicule of the Lexicon, upon which he had never ceased to labour, which took place in 1961 shortly after he had moved.

Ask anyone who knew him during this period (whether a member of the academic or administrative staff or a student), and the verdict will be unanimous: he gave the constant impression of kindness, concern, and good will. When he moved on, there was general regret at his going.

6
CAMBRIDGE

In the Cambridge period, Geoffrey Lampe accumulated so many responsibilities that it is difficult to understand how he could have discharged them all successfully. Yet, any one of the following tributes, if isolated, might lead the reader to imagine that his only concern was the one being described: so remarkably did he give himself wholly to the matter in hand.

An estimate of him as a theologian by Dr George Newlands is followed by Professor Gordon Rupp's 'Board's Eye View' and an evaluation by Professor Henry Chadwick of the Patristic Lexicon and Lampe's part in its making. Then come Dr Sealy's account of him as a Fellow of Caius, Mr Andrew's tribute to his work on the Board of Extra-mural Studies, Bishop Roberts on his Ely canonry, Lord Coggan on his contribution to General Synod, and a narrative of the Anglo-Scandinavian conversations by Canon David Isitt and Professor Lars Oesterlin.

AS A THEOLOGIAN

by the Reverend G. M. Newlands, BD, PhD

Doctor Newlands is a University Lecturer in Divinity at Cambridge, and a Fellow of Wolfson College. Before this, he was a Lecturer in Theology at Glasgow. He graduated from Edinburgh, of which he holds the MA, BD, and PhD, and was Ordained into the Ministry of the Church of Scotland in1970. After Geoffrey Lampe's death, he edited a collection of his essays, *Explorations in Theology*, 8, 1981.

I

Geoffrey Lampe came to the Ely Chair of Divinity in Cambridge in 1959. Already an established scholar, he had succeeded in combining a multitude of pastoral and administrative duties in Oxford and Birmingham with a range of publications which, solid rather than voluminous, was to provide a secure basis for his future research. The subjects dealt with echo almost precisely the later academic interests, and provide the contours of a programme which was to be developed with formidable energy, a delicious sense of humour and always a daunting professional expertise.

Cambridge theology has taken on many different colours over the years but it has not been without distinctive character. The tradition of Erasmus, Ridley and Bucer, of Lightfoot, Westcott and Hort, has never been afraid to follow truth wherever it might lead, and to speak the truth boldly in love as the open invitation of God's love. It is my brief in this paper to confine myself to Geoffrey Lampe's theology. But his theology is perhaps best understood against the background of a keen participation in the affairs of the university, in politics and education in the region, and of a strong and constantly renewed sense of the life and worship of the Church. Not for nothing was he a canon and an honorary canon of Ely, and a devoted chairman of the council of Westcott House and member of the council of Ridley Hall. This was a passion for Athens and for Jerusalem, for the one precisely because of the other, expressed in a distinctive style. Here was humour without frivolity, commitment with a wide tolerance of other points of view, bold experiment in faith with deeply serious intention. 'Having God, he had all, and, held by God, he knew what real security means.' (Charlie Moule).

'What in all this he was concerned for was that God *himself*, and not another, had acted in love in the human scene.' (Peter Walker).

II

In 1948 there appeared in the *Journal of Theological Studies* a couple of articles by G. W. H. Lampe on patristic discussion of Baptism. There followed essays on the meaning of the Christian ministry and the significance of Word and Sacrament, culminating in the definitive study of Baptism in the early Church, *The Seal of the Spirit*, of 1951. The Spirit of God is the keystone, or rather the constantly moving impulse, of the whole corpus of Professor Lampe's writing. Concern for Baptism was linked to concern for Confirmation and to the whole question of ministry. Though we shall look in vain for ecumenical jargon in Lampe's work, concern for the unity of the Church was a major spring of his creative effort. The roots of this may lie in the war years, in Birmingham, and in aspects of his whole life and theology, and will no doubt suffer the usual fate of becoming a suitable research topic for a higher degree. This ecumenical engagement provoked a stream of papers on Church and ministry, ordination and intercommunion, and a notable participation in the Open Letter about the Church in South India. Beyond ecumenism came a catholic interest in God as the reconciler of all mankind who invites us to participate in mystery without mystification and in rationality without rationalism. The unemployed and the socially disadvantaged were in, exorcists and the Moonies were out.

Apart from the work on Church and Sacraments and on the Holy Spirit, especially in the writing of his favourite evangelist, St Luke, the Birmingham years brought a study of Luther and of the doctrine of justification by faith. This wrestling with the heritage of the Reformation was to stand Lampe in good stead in twenty years of work with the Anglo-Scandinavian conversations. It was to come out, too, in his understanding of grace in the development of his Christology, to be summed up in the first instance in *Reconciliation in Christ*, the F. D. Maurice lectures for 1955. The terms God and Christ were never to be alternatives, and so neither Barthian Christomonism nor deistic unitarianism could hold much attraction—though charity would lead him to contribute to a collection of essays in honour of Karl Barth. The search for criteria brought up sharply the question of authority. How was the freedom of the Spirit to be related to the letter of the sacred text? A provisional answer was forthcoming in essays on scripture and tradition, on authority, and, with Kenneth Woollcombe, in *Essays in Typology*, 1957.

III

The first years in Ely saw publications spanning both the patristic and modern periods, discussion of creeds in the Fathers and the credo *I Believe* in the present, the Patristic Greek Lexicon and some short plays for children for the BBC. The juxtaposition of the Fathers and the present day has always been characteristic of the Anglican tradition. Lampe had added Luther, and the Scandinavian connection kept up this concern. In discussing the sacramental tradition he did not forget the medievals. If there was a gap it was perhaps in the spirit of St Thomas, though he was to attempt always to include the Roman Catholic tradition in the enterprises with which he sought renewed understanding and fellowship. This was a time of more articles on the ministry, the eucharist, and especially on the authority of the Bible in the modern world, together with the chapters on Luke and Acts for the new version of *Peake's Commentary*. The results for his theology of this scholarly activity can be well seen in *The Resurrection*, a dialogue with D. M. MacKinnon, 1966.

The dialogue arose from *An Easter Sermon* [to which reference has already been made by Canon Purcell, pp. 9 ff. above]. Geoffrey Lampe preached a large number of sermons, often to undergraduates, with a light touch and in a matter-of-fact style. He wanted to communicate with ordinary intelligent people, and he was deeply suspicious of anything in theology which he could not commend succinctly and intelligibly to the man or woman in the pew. Lampe always bore in mind the sort of comments that his old friend Donald MacKinnon would make, especially when he knew that they would not be of approval. There were others too—I mention only C. F. D. Moule, whose New Testament seminar kept the Cambridge biblical tradition at the centre of the enterprise, and Gordon Rupp, whose gentle humour provided the perfect mirror for ecumenical speculation. Lampe provided a curious unifying influence, being precisely himself rather than all things to all men, and inviting others to be themselves. Fair and tolerant almost to a fault, he assumed the same qualities in others as a matter of course. The sermon begins with Paul's preaching of the Risen Christ. 'The real Christ is not a revived corpse. He lives in the fullness of God's life. He is the life, the truth, the way for us. He lives for us and in us.' We must not ask for the wrong sort of proof. 'There was no objective demonstration at Easter that Jesus had won the victory. He was never seen by Caiaphas or Pilate or the Jerusalem mob. . . . There is no proof of that kind. Only the assurance of experience.' This was not a message of simple optimism. 'Easter does not guarantee an easy comfortable time all round. On the contrary, the unquenched light of the world shines most brightly in the long line of the martyrs, from Peter and Paul at Rome in the year 65 or thereabouts to James Reeb in . . . Alabama, in the year 1965.'

In the discussion Lampe says of the Resurrection that 'It is an assertion that is possible only to faith. But faith makes this assertion on the basis of certain things that are recorded as having actually happened at Easter.' He saw Christian experience of resurrection as 'a real encounter with an objective presence'. Professor MacKinnon had approached the matter in 1953 from a rather different angle. 'At the heart of human history, then, stands for the Christian the agony, the struggle of Christ . . . It is deed: not idea.' He later noted that 'It is because I seek after *facts* . . . that I look for a publicly observable state of affairs in the spatial and temporal world, not disclosing, nor containing, but still pointing towards (in a way that I agree remains entirely ambivalent) that which is, in my view, necessarily *unique* and creative'.

Among great differences there are remarkable convergences. Neither is looking for unmistakable signs. Both stress the primacy of faith, Lampe in the absence of visible signs and MacKinnon in the ambivalent nature of the facts. Both affirm the Resurrection as an event that happened in the public world, and both reject the existentialist understanding of resurrection as myth in a purely subjective interpretation. For MacKinnon the heart of the matter is the deed done in the active obedience of Christ. For Lampe it is the act of grace in reconciliation through the cross, the response of faith through the Spirit and the sealing of commitment in Christian martyrdom. The most striking aspect of this dialogue, at a time of the almost complete conversion of continental theology to the school of Rudolf Bultmann and the wave of secular theology which followed the publication of *Honest to God* in Britain, is the considerable caution which both scholars exercise in relation to the classical Christian tradition. The Anglican communion has always been much concerned with the ancient creeds in its life and worship. (A minister of the Kirk may perhaps recall in brief piety that Calvin thought creeds delightful if not overdone, though he inevitably denied any such licence to others.) The subject of ingenious revision, radical rejection and glorious reaffirmation, the patristic legacy remains important as a link with the Christian past and a source of new creative reflection in the present.

IV

The next decade brought a number of extremely interesting essays. *The God of the Christians* (from *The Phenomenon of Christian Belief*, 1970) is a persuasive suggestion that trustful confidence in God's grace has nothing whatever to do with clutching at infallibilities, whether in books, formulas, or institutions. *The Limuru Principle and Church Unity* (1974, reprinted in *Explorations in Theology*, 8, 1981) extends the same dogmatic judgement to the nitty-gritty (as Donald MacKinnon might have called it) of the validity of non-episcopal ordination. *The Holy Spirit and the Person of Christ* is an important essay in Christology. The continuing freshness of the argument, despite being the subject of a decade's weary sackfuls of examination scripts, is a tribute to its quality. Even for an endlessly patient advocate like Lampe there comes a point when the fact of spiritual experience, like the universe, just has to be accepted. 'If God has, as it appears, willed that his Spirit should communicate with men and inspire them through Christ, that is, by witnessing to Christ and referring to him as the archetype and norm, then this is a fact of God's dealings with men which it would be profitless to question. Like his election of Israel, it has to be accepted.' At the same time, not out of diffidence but out of due regard for the role of the theologian as a worker *with others* he ends on a note not of apostrophe but of self-interrogation. 'Or must Spirit christology after all give way at this point to the concept of the incarnation of the pre-existent divine being, the Logos/Son?'

Christian Believing, a report by the Doctrine Commission of the Church of England, was dear to Geoffrey Lampe's heart, and his response to criticism was not to retract but to wait for and to expect better times. Produced by a very diverse group, the report's statements inevitably sacrifice something for linguistic unanimity. The individual essays are powerful pleas in favour of particular points of view. Lampe produced the Appendix on *The Origins of the Creeds*. It was quite clear to him, standing in a long scholarly tradition, that the origins and purposes of the creeds were often entirely different from those romantically imagined by theologians in whom weight of pious learning overcame critical judgement.

In his individual essay Geoffrey Lampe took up the report's theme of the Christian life as a voyage of discovery, a quest, an adventure. Revelation never comes neat and undiluted, in Bible, Church, or historical events. Concepts of authority change, but there remains 'the essentially unchanging human experience of being encountered by God . . . The centre and heart of this continuing encounter between God and man is, as I believe, Jesus Christ.' The Christian sacraments 'signify, evoke and sustain our experience of living at the present time in the Spirit of Christ' as we await God's final transformation in the Spirit.

Geoffrey would have been the first to agree that the story of human salvation has many different facets. Sometimes God's grace is experienced as a great release, when all attempt at discovery, initiative, and activity has failed, when people are broken in circumstances of mindless evil, cruelty, or futility. Here the memory of a deed done may become the centre of salvation. When the plausibility criteria of the present become too constricting, strange chords from the past may stimulate new perspectives. Sometimes the voyage of discovery may begin to resemble a pleasure cruise for successful people in a sea of structural alienation and unemployment. Geoffrey could see this, and still take delight in the sight of a small chorus leaning daringly overboard to mutter Marxist incantations of woe, while safely contriving never to fall off the first class deck. He well knew the danger of narcissism in any institution, and the other side of his vision is the large collection of sermons on Christian discipleship, very often taken up with specific practical, political, and social issues.

In 1939, when William Temple produced his admirable *Doctrine in the Church of England* there was still a certain consensus that profound experience of transcendence was to be referred to the religious dimension, to Christianity and the Church. By 1976 things had changed: the God of Hastings Rashdall was as remote as the God of Cyril of Alexandria. Idealism was out, and critical realism was not necessarily successful either. The *fact* of Christian experience of the Spirit was not universally admissible or even conceivable. Nevertheless, for Lampe this was not to be the signal for a return to the primrose path of Nicaeno-Constantinopolitan rectitude.

V

In November 1977 there appeared from the Clarendon Press *God as Spirit*, the Bampton Lectures for 1976. On the first pages were the names of Augustine and Charles Raven. Raven and Augustine were men who knew the world of affairs and attempted to speak in universal terms without compromising the Gospel. Both were capable of breathtaking doctrinal innovation, and could easily in another age have come to a sticky or uncomfortably crisp end. The names pointed to a serious and comprehensive intention in the catholic tradition, and should alert us against any suggestion of an *agōnisma es to parachrēma*.

God as Spirit has been much reviewed and discussed. Reading again the first chapters four years on one is struck by the high incidence of biblical language. This may be seen as a precritical limitation. It may also indicate a mature employment of biblical language as an appropriate medium for doing theology. That I think is how Lampe saw the internal structure of *God as Spirit*, based as it largely was on the Bible and the Fathers. He saw the natural medium of theological discourse not in an ultra-modern hermeneutical repristination of medieval metaphysics, but in an informed and controlled employment of ordinary language. It would have been interesting to relate his narrative to all sorts of possibly cognate areas from the sociology of knowledge to the semiotic structure of Robbe-Grillet's novels. But it was not necessary. Frenetic search for exotic clothes is sometimes a sign of intellectual nakedness. He knew exactly what he was doing and why. Here was the learned simplicity which is one of the great strengths of his style.

A selection of quotations will perhaps exhibit some of the building blocks. ' "Incarnation" and "inspiration" are not in fact two quite different alternative models for Christology. Inspiration . . . must convey the deeper meaning of a "real presence" of God himself. Incarnation, unless understood in inspirational terms, is equally inadequate.' An apparently easy target for conservative critics of various varieties in the *Myth of God Incarnate* controversy, Lampe always seemed to have moved on just a fraction when the smoke cleared.

'We are not saved by an event as such, not even the event of Good Friday, but by its effect upon us when it is interpreted in a certain way.' Here we seem to be in the presence of pure subjectivism, from which we may be instantly rescued by the reflection that we are saved, by definition, only by God. Through grace the continuities between various parts of acts and events come to have human significance in ways complex beyond our imagining. In the Logos theology which was the basis of the traditional doctrine of the Trinity, 'The characteristic features of the life of Jesus, especially his relationship to God, are read back into the eternal relationship of the hypostatized and anthropomorphically conceived Logos-Wisdom of the Father': none of which is particularly helpful. Resurrection is not a return of Jesus to friends who had let him down but 'a taking up of those friends, and of all subsequent believers, into his life of sonship. . . . Belief in future life did not depend for the first Christians, and need not for ourselves, upon an Easter event. It rests upon the trust which believers place in the faithfulness of God; on their assurance of the creative presence of God the Spirit.' True realism is found not only in the intellectual but also in the practical resolution. Grace is given in being given away and truth is apprehended in doing the truth. Resurrection is appropriated in fulfilment of the life of sonship with Christ.

'I believe that the Trinitarian model is in the end less satisfactory for the articulation of our basic Christian experience than the unifying concept of God as Spirit.' 'It is to express the concept of the immanent creative activity of the transcendent Creator that we use the term "Spirit", referring to the one God, transcendent and immanent, as he makes himself known in his outgoing towards us which is also his indwelling within us.'

Lampe has been described as a heretic and a deist, usually by opponents and sometimes by admirers. He did indeed offer radical modification of traditional doctrine, though always as a faithful son of the Church. To find heresy where there is no heretical intention may itself be somewhat heretical. He was not a deist in the sense of preferring a *principium* of the Father and a subordination of the Son and the Spirit. If he had felt that continuity with classical unitarianism was best he would have said so plainly. I shall not rehearse a Hesiodic catalogue of possible heresies.

VI

God as Spirit was written not to be worshipped but to be used. Observing that classical trinitarians have sometimes been unable either to forget anything or to learn anything, Lampe perhaps underrated the intellectual challenge of the trinitarian option in the present. Like Schleiermacher he had very good reasons for bracketing out the trinitarian dimension, regarding the *filioque* controversy, the very model of a modern ecumenical agenda, as much ado about nothing. Some things are better discarded than endlessly refurbished. It may be that trinitarian theology, unlike other traditional doctrines, is saved by the fact that it does continue to commend itself from the reflection on Christian experience which Geoffrey so emphasised. But if so, adequate reformulation will not come through Byzantine reiteration.

Hegel's heirs, notably in Process theology, have rather liked the Trinity: Schleiermacher's have not been so certain. But things are not so simple. For David Jenkins the Trinity is of the essence, for Hendrikus Berkhof it is not. Distinctions for exellence and dullness can be fairly equally divided between trinitarian and non-trinitarian theologies. The God who is a living fire and a refuge for the weary and the heavy laden is not easily expressed in our concepts. Much depends on the nature of the specification. The God of the Christians I understand as one who is in his essential nature love, love characterised precisely and uniquely in the self-giving of God to mankind in the events surrounding the life, death, and resurrection of Jesus of Nazareth. It is not *so* difficult to produce an intellectually respectable account of God as a transcendent source of self-giving love: the problems arise in the scandal of particularity.

Much in the tradition was docetic and obscurantist. Lampe sought renewal by making pneumatology the centre of theology. He concentrated on the anthropological rather than the cosmological dimension of creation and reconciliation, seeing man always as God's man, through the Spirit, and ordinary language as a check on escape into the realm of speculation, which he regarded as a form of cheap grace. Two thousand years of doctrinal tradition are a fraction only of the history of creation, and faith is always led on to seek deeper understanding. In *God as Spirit* we may find an invaluable clue to further exploration.

Part of the foundation for this profound study has now appeared in the long section on *Christian Theology in the Patristic Period*, contributed to the History of Christian Doctrine ed. H. Cunliffe-Jones (1978). Based on the witty and challenging lectures from which generations of undergraduates in Cambridge and Birmingham learned much of their theology, it is constantly enlivened by the keen theological interest throughout. The Patristics card game can be played by the expert in an unlimited number of combinations to produce fury, vexation, and delight. And for the Christian tradition there is more to the Fathers than cards. These lectures over the years constituted a significant event. But as the first rule of Geoffrey Lampe's theology reminds us, events without interpretation and further engagement remain powerless. We begin to learn only as we are open to invitation.

Through books and lectures, articles and sermons, parties and quiet conversations, we may count ourselves uniquely privileged to have shared the company of a man who was wise and generous and good, and who could sum up our faith and our ultimate hope in this way: 'I believe in the Divinity of our Lord and Saviour Jesus Christ, in the sense that the one God, the Creator and Saviour Spirit, revealed himself and acted decisively for us in Jesus. I believe in the Divinity of the Holy Ghost, in the sense that the same one God, the Creator and Saviour Spirit, is here and now not far from every one of us; for in him we live and move, in him we have our being, in us, if we consent to know him and trust him, he will create the Christlike harvest: love, joy, peace, patience, kindness, goodness, fidelity, gentleness, and self-control.'

A BOARD'S EYE VIEW

by the Reverend Professor E. G. Rupp, DD, FBA

Professor Rupp, who is in retirement at Cambridge, was Professor of Church History at Manchester and the Dixie Professor at Cambridge and a Fellow of Emmanuel College. He is a former President of the Methodist Conference, and a world authority on Reformation history and theology and the author of works especially in this field.

The Cambridge Divinity Faculty is small, but its faculty board has a century of honourable history. As a governing body it has been consistently good tempered, and its members—if the old phrase be permitted— Christian gentlemen. The decorum of its venue, the Lightfoot Room, with its portrait of the great 'J.B.' and of F. J. A. Hort, serves it in the office of a wall against the kind of rumpuses, and waspish encounters which may seem to go on elsewhere. Traditionally, the four Divinity professors count for much, so that of necessity Geoffrey Lampe, as Ely and Regius Professor, was prominent in its doings.

A 'board's eye view' of a theologian must be relatively unexciting, since for most of us, attendance at committees belongs to the chores rather than the amenities of academic existence. None the less, you cannot sit opposite to anybody regularly for several years without glimpses of temperament and character which remain as friendly and valued memories. Geoffrey chaired meetings with unfailing courtesy and quiet humour. And sitting opposite him in a Degree committee, when somebody was rather going on and on, and one longed for a burbling voice to cease and wondered if it ever would, it was a relief to catch Geoffrey's eye, and note the raised eyebrows and the twinkle, and for me patience would be restored.

The smaller sub-committees are often important, a Degree committee or an examiners' meeting, much more than a flourish of papers, for at stake might be the happiness and future of applicants, of candidates, and of those whose dissertations were weighed in the balance. And there were the rather nice committees where one gave away other people's money, where tricky decisions had sometimes to be made, and the more awesome Appointments committee where

Lecturers might be made. Whether as chairman or as a member of those committees, he would not speak much but would often speak decisively, and I can say this because, though I generally agreed with what he said, I hardly ever seemed to vote as he did.

One has many memories of the road from the Divinity school— of meeting one another as each breasted a contrary stream of tourists, undergraduates, and shoppers, or darted across the traffic into Heffer's. Just inside Mowbray's there is a stand for religious newspapers and periodicals, and both he and I had a habit of standing before it and musing at the proffered fare, generally without buying anything, and on his face the kind of sceptical wonder which recalled the famous cartoon of Mr Gladstone looking at one of Disraeli's novels and murmuring 'Prosy!' For while he was immersed in what is called 'the contemporary dialogue' there was in him an independence which came from love of truth, and a courage to be against the received opinions, entirely free from any desire to titillate or to shock, '*pour épater les bourgeois*'. And there was one afternoon when he was rumoured to be ill, when he came in having been caught without an overcoat in a great rain, near Wandlebury, and had strode the miles to get back to the Divinity school peacefully unruffled and seeming almost to have enjoyed what for most of us would have been an irritating and tiresome experience.

Goodness and kindness, humour and courage, these do not need the great occasions, or the grand assemblies, for their revelation. Looking back, the good small talk of little meetings have been the sacraments, the affectionate tokens, of a beloved and honoured colleague.

THE PATRISTIC GREEK LEXICON

by the Reverend Professor H. Chadwick, DD, MusB, FBA

Professor Chadwick has recently returned to Cambridge as Regius Professor of Divinity and is a Fellow of Magdalene College. After some years in Cambridge as a Fellow of Queens' College and a University Lecturer, he was appointed Regius Professor of Divinity at Oxford and then Dean of Christ Church.

The *Patristic Greek Lexicon* (Clarendon Press, 1961–8, and subsequent reprints) is a large volume packed with weighty information, and bears Geoffrey Lampe's name on the title-page with good reason. His was the dynamic editorial mind which applied the indispensable force to bring half a century of work to a conclusion. He knew it to be in important respects a provisional conclusion; but without him the book would very probably not have come to be.

The Lexicon began as far back as 1906 at Cambridge on the impetus of the Regius Professor, Henry Barclay Swete, gentlest of wise and indefatigable scholars, whose organising energy and powers of persuasion fostered and often originated vital causes (such as the *Journal of Theological Studies*, only one among his notable brainchildren). He had a charisma for bringing learned men together in unwonted co-operation. From the start he was enthusiastically supported by Canon Herbert Moore. But the first formally appointed editor was the Principal of Pusey House, Darwell Stone, nominated to edit the Lexicon in 1915. His reign lasted twenty-five years, and far from negligible work was done in his time. Simultaneously Sir Henry Stuart Jones was engaged on the ninth edition of 'Liddell and Scott' (LSJ), which appeared in fascicles from 1925 to 1940. Unlike Liddell's eighth edition (1897) in which some patristic usages are recorded, the ninth edition of LSJ excluded all Christian texts other than, paradoxically, the New Testament. Even a writer as undistinctively Christian as Synesius is excluded on the sole ground of his beliefs, though everything else about him would make his vocabulary a source of much illumination for LSJ. LSJ deliberately left the Christians to Stone. Stone himself was widely read in the pages of Migne and at Pusey House had beside him an excellent patristic library. But he and not a few of his assistants (often, like Moore, high Anglican country clergy of a generation that had enjoyed a first-rate classical education) saw their task much more in theological than in philological terms. Their ideas were in obvious respects akin to those motivating Gerhard Kittel's *Theological Dictionary of the New Testament*, and certainly nearer to Kittel than to Walter Bauer. Other assistants, however, saw their role as simple recorders of linguistic usage, and these readers could fail to spot passages of high dogmatic interest, just as some of the more theologically-minded readers of the texts could be blind to an unusual word or turn of phrase or to one with a philosophical background.

Stone died in 1940, and the editorship passed to his friend and biographer Frank Leslie Cross (1900–68), a scholar of steel whose encyclopaedic interests came to be faithfully mirrored in his indispensable *Oxford Dictionary of the Christian Church* (1st edition, 1957). Leslie Cross was extremely reticent and shy, but possessed in a rare degree both imagination and organising energy (as his series of Patristic Conferences from 1951 onwards bear witness). His imagination was always vulnerable to being fired by new vistas of unexplored territory. I recall Norman Baynes, who was excited by Cross's Oxford inaugural on Athanasius, expressing to me his regret that it had not led on to a big book and that 'the path behind this most learned man was strewn with unweaned babies'. Cross was liable to take up a new project before the old could be brought to a decisive conclusion. But his imagination and critical grasp gave him a genius for writing a programmatic statement of work needing to be done, incisively setting out the principles which should govern the operation. He was editor of the Lexicon only until 1948, but it fell to him firmly to articulate the twin objectives of the book being planned, namely that the PGL should give the fullest treatment to words important for Christian theology, liturgy, and institutions, and that simultaneously it should provide a linguistic supplement to LSJ. Cross drew up the valuable prefatory list of authors and works.

The material available on the slips in the Lexicon filing cabinets varied considerably in quality according to the eye of the reader assigned to any given author. Clement of Alexandria, Eusebius, and Dionysius the Areopagite were certainly read by experts; the Cappadocian Fathers and John Chrysostom are handled in the Lexicon reasonably well, but not quite at the same high level of observation. Both Stone and Cross were especially interested in what is distinctively Christian, and therefore tended not to require their readers to note instances of religious or ethical language used in patristic authors which was already part of the common vocabulary of antiquity for these subjects. Under Stone the acute mind of Leonard Prestige (1889–1955) was enlisted to bring order to the main technical terms of Trinitarian and Christological debate. But neither Cross nor Stone saw the Lexicon's task as the vigilant collection of, say, the colloquialisms characteristic of the anecdotes of John Moschus or culled from the plentiful folklore of the Acta Sanctorum.

Geoffrey Lampe joined in the work of the Lexicon under Cross's leadership on his taking up his work at St John's after the war. Already Cross had begun to gather a larger team of helpers. Miss H. C. Graef came and did sterling work. Cross recruited a major figure in the Lexicon's making when in 1946 he persuaded Mary Grosvenor (now of the Pontifical Biblical Institute) to come from Edinburgh. The preface to the published Lexicon bears eloquent testimony to the crucial contribution that she made. She saw that the Lexicon needed not only decisive rulings on style of references for the sake of consistency but also a 'philosophy' of professional lexicography. A public lecture by C. T. Onions providentially occurred at just the time when the new team was in search of expert methodological guidance. Geoffrey Lampe took over the responsibilities of the editorship in 1948. Leslie Cross's interests were already beginning to move away towards the construction of his great *Dictionary*. Geoffrey's advent brought fresh energy to the project. With his usual fund of practical common sense he at once realised that, if it was not to wander on timelessly, the Lexicon needed a much enlarged team of scholarly assistants, free to work in Oxford as a team, and therefore that great efforts must be made to raise considerable extra sums to pay their salaries. Substantial subscriptions were contributed by Oxford and Cambridge colleges, by cathedrals, and others, including private individuals. The assistants, at one time as many as eleven, came from a wide variety of backgrounds and ecclesiastical allegiances. They not only had to know the languages, but also had to work with a high degree of objectivity in controversial areas. Some were temporarily unemployed academics, others people who had tried the religious life and withdrawn from it, others still refugees from the blackboard jungle of schoolteaching. Father (now Archbishop) Basil Krivocheine added a distinctive feature. At one time a lay Russian monk on Mount Athos, he had suffered internment in Greece when a Russian connection was suspect, and was helped to come to England by Bishop George Bell so that he could help with the Lexicon. The Bodleian provided a large room, and a working library was assembled (Cuddesdon College generously lent Migne).

Most of these assistants, wittily and affectionately known as 'the Slaves of the Lampe', worked full-time. Geoffrey, however, had heavy duties in his college and in faculty teaching. He gave every spare moment he had to the Lexicon, and startled his helpers by his ability to use even a twenty-minute gap advantageously by taking the slips to draft some short article. Articles on major theological themes were written by him or by Hilda Graef or Mary Grosvenor, and (as Geoffrey came to realise that even among the assistants he had recruited there were variations in ability) only minor articles could be delegated to more junior helpers. His concentrated energy, determination, and capacity for rapid working inspired the entire team with a sense of dedication and of the importance of their common task. Every summer Geoffrey and Elizabeth gave the team a delectable picnic in Bagley Wood, to all a most memorable event.

Because financial support at the requisite level was unlikely to be forthcoming for more than a few years, Geoffrey and his team were faced with some painful problems. As they worked on the drafting of the articles, it became clear that some of the old material in the filing cabinets was of indifferent quality, and that a number of texts (especially ascetic and hagiographical texts with small dogmatic interest but much to tell the student of vocabulary, grammar, and syntax) had not been slipped at all. The team therefore tried to supplement and improve the material at the same time as it was being ordered into shape for the printer. As the work came to near its final stages, there was something of a crisis of confidence. At the end of the day would the Delegates of the Oxford University Press, who had been cautiously supportive and encouraging throughout but uncommitted, finally judge that the result of all this labour would be of a sufficiently high standard of scholarship to merit their jealously guarded imprint? Would it be worthy to stand beside 'Liddell-Scott-Jones', to which it was intended as a supplement? Geoffrey Lampe knew better than anyone that, were he allowed time and money, a substantially better book could be produced. But time and money were both likely to be severely limited, and at least what had been done on the theological side was obviously of high quality. Geoffrey Lampe himself was responsible for the big articles on all words connected with baptism and Christian initiation, material which his book *The Seal of the Spirit* (1951) surveyed in a wider context; he also wrote *monogenes* and *huios*. But was the work as a whole now ready for public criticism? The Delegates were naturally aware that the quality of the work stretching over many years was uneven. It was their duty to express hesitations. In the end numerous cardboard boxes containing the completed work were brought over in a van from the Oxford University Press to Cambridge where the Delegates sought an independent critical opinion. The final advice was clear and in the event justified. Granted that there were many unevennesses and incompletenesses, nevertheless it would be a tragic setback if all that had been achieved were to remain unpublished; and, above all, in Geoffrey Lampe the Delegates could look to an editor with good scholarly equipment especially in the theological ideas which were central to the matter of the Lexicon. The decision to go ahead was in no small measure a vote of confidence in the judgement, learning, and good sense of the editor.

The years immediately following the Second World War saw a vigorous efflorescence of patristic studies. Critical editions and learned monographs quickly increased in number under the converging currents of different influences. Classical scholars were looking about in late antiquity for new historical and literary problems to solve. Theologians were seeking a fresh impulse, notably under the impact of the ecumenical movement, to return to the sources behind the schematised scholastic systems of Reformation and Counter-Reformation. The French Jesuits launched 'Sources Chrétiennes'. Altaner's *Patrology* appeared in much revised form in 1950. In 1951 Leslie Cross master-minded the first Patristic Conference at Christ Church. When the first of the five fascicles of the Lexicon appeared in 1961, the book came to a learned world hungrily crying out for it; and the OUP was able to publish the successive parts with astonishing speed and accuracy, at what now seems an almost give-away price. For what it is the book must be deemed inexpensive at its 1981 price of £60.

The strength and toughness of the PGL lie in its masterly treatment of the basic vocabulary of Christian theology, liturgy, ethics, and social institutions. At the same time the fundamental decision of principle to plan the work as a supplement to LSJ, while very intelligible and practical, has certain disadvantages whose force is more and more felt as one uses it. Just as LSJ suffers from the exclusion of a writer such as Synesius merely on the ground that this impassioned Neoplatonist became a Christian, and a bishop at that, so inversely, like a mirror-image, PGL suffers from its rigid limitation to Christian authors. One result is that it is hard to see what is specifically Christian language in comparison with the usage of contemporary pagan writers. One cannot discover from PGL how or when Christian writers used words that were already part of the normal classical vocabulary and are therefore recorded in LSJ but often for the later period in only a partial and fragmentary way. And in view of the predominantly theological interest of the work, it is perhaps surprising that, except for *epi*, relatively little attention is given to prepositions; after all, the question whether or not one may rightly say '*in* two natures' has divided Christendom. ('In' has also had its troubles in post-Reformation eucharistic controversies.) PGL has no article *en*.

It would be misleading, however, to describe the PGL as a book whose weaknesses must irritate the philologically-minded scholar. The article on *hina* is, I think, a masterly survey of the ways in which this word came to be used in late Greek, and contains material observations simply not to be found elsewhere. The first three fascicles were given full reviews in the *JTS* at the hand of the brilliant Swedish philologist, the late Albert Wifstrand of Lund. His admiration for the theological articles was unqualified; and he was not in doubt that, while there are many gaps and even minor mistakes in the treatment of other words, the work is an indispensable reference work and one for which the student of the Greek language, without specially theological interests, has reason to be deeply grateful. Without Geoffrey Lampe's work as editor—an outstanding instance of the right man in the right place at the right time—it is most unlikely it would have seen the light.

(I have to thank Miss Mary D. Grosvenor, Miss Noël Butler-Wright, and Miss Mary Cunningham for sharing with me some of their memories of working as members of the team of assistants on the Lexicon.)

AS A FELLOW OF CAIUS COLLEGE

by L. S. Sealy, PhD

Doctor Sealy is a University Lecturer in Law at Cambridge, and has been a Fellow of Gonville and Caius College since 1959. He was brought up in New Zealand, where he practised Law for a time, but most of his career has been as an academic.

When one asks his colleagues, as I have recently been doing, what they remember of Geoffrey Lampe as a Fellow of Caius, the striking thing is that they don't—what they invariably recall and dwell upon is Geoffrey the man. It is the large-hearted friend, the warm personality, the merry companion, the generous host, that stands out in the memory; the Christian who lived his beliefs but (except from the pulpit) did not preach them; the scholar whose learning was rich and deep and wide but was never idly flaunted; the colleague who gave his friendship freely to all of us, asking nothing more in return than the chance to get to know each of us better. And so, although the story which I am about to tell is of a Fellow who served the College in many capacities and who played a leading part in its affairs, it is a story of one who did not seek power in office or covet the limelight, the counsellor whose opinion often prevailed although he never sought to push his views, the Caian for whom what mattered above all was the college community itself and its wellbeing. In other words, it is just one part of the story of Geoffrey the man.

It would no doubt be wrong to assume that he was altogether a stranger to Cambridge when he arrived here in 1959 to take up the Ely Professorship of Divinity in the University, but it is certainly true that most of his academic life prior to that date had been spent on the further side of Bletchley railway junction, and that he had no special connection with any Cambridge college. A new Chair at Oxford carries with it automatically a Fellowship at a designated college; but at Cambridge the bureaucratic game known as the 'quota' system puts new arrivals into a kind of lottery. It was good luck for us at Caius that we happened to be below our quota and so free to make an offer to the new Ely Professor, and a happy coincidence that the Dean of Caius at that time was Hugh Montefiore (now Bishop of Birmingham) who had formerly been Geoffrey's pupil at St John's College, Oxford, and thus someone well placed to make the introduction. So it was that in the summer of 1960 the Council of Caius resolved to elect Geoffrey Lampe into a Professorial Fellowship, and that shortly afterwards he made in the College chapel, in the presence of the Master and assembled Fellows, the traditional declaration required by the College statutes of a new Fellow. This is formulated in vague and curiously subjective terms: he must promise to discharge the duties of a Fellow of the College 'to the best of my judgement and ability'. There is nothing anywhere to give the novice Fellow more specific guidance; but in the last couple of decades there could not have been better advice given to any other young don than to model his ways on those of Geoffrey Lampe.

Few university posts put upon their incumbent such a weight of potentially conflicting duties as does the Ely Chair of Divinity. First and foremost, there are of course the teaching and administrative commitments as a professor; but at the same time, as a member of the Chapter at Ely and a resident within the precincts of the cathedral, there are very many calls from that quarter. Alone amongst all Cambridge dons, the Ely Professor has a statutory *obligation* to commute, over a distance of some seventeen miles. How this was worked out in earlier times when man was so dependent upon the horse is something I have often wondered about (although one can say in passing, so far as Geoffrey was concerned, that it would not have been beyond either his skills or his resources to have made the journey by pony and trap even in the 1960s!); but today it simply means that the Professor has a schedule obliging him to motor back and forth, sometimes more than once in a day, frequently in bad weather, and as often as not in a hurry.

So placed, and having in addition his work as a scholar, his writings and sermons, and the calls of home and family, it would have been reasonable enough for a Fellow in Geoffrey's position to have allowed the College to make minimal claims on his time and energies: to have dropped in for lunch when that happened to be convenient, brought in a guest occasionally to dinner, and little more. But this was not Geoffrey's way. The College became his principal place of study and work, and over the years he brought in books in such quantities that his needs in bookshelves became legendary. Far from opting out of college commitments, he seems to have gone out of his way to find roles in which he could be of service.

All the more important corporate decisions are taken at Caius by a Council consisting of the Master and twelve Fellows. Geoffrey was elected to this body within two years of his arrival, and had a place on it throughout the greater part of his time as a Fellow. Like many academic committees, the Council is not noted for reaching its conclusions speedily, or at all times in a cool and orderly manner; but Geoffrey was, in my recollection, outstandingly the member who stood apart from the rest of us in not showing such donnish failings. His contributions to the discussion were rare, and characteristically thoughtful, brief, and full of good sense; most often, he offered no opinion unless asked for it; he was never partisan, always objective, with a concern for what was practicable, what was humane, what would keep things running on an even keel.

On two occasions when the secretary of the Council, the College Registrary, was away on sabbatical leave, Geoffrey stood in for him. This meant tons of correspondence and committee-work, and made many demands on stamina, patience, and tact. It is remarkable that one with so many other commitments should have found time to undertake this task at all; but it will be no surprise to those who knew Geoffrey to learn that he discharged its many burdens effectively and with much good will.

In October 1963, Hugh Montefiore left his university post and his office as Dean of Caius to become Vicar of the University Church, Great St Mary's. (Thence to Kingston-upon-Thames, where at his enthronement the college was represented by a number of Fellows, and he was attended by more than one former Chaplain of Caius, on an occasion at which Geoffrey Lampe preached a memorable sermon.) It was natural enough that the College should ask Geoffrey to serve on the committee appointed to consider filling the vacancy. But it was surely beyond anyone's conception of the call of duty that, when it turned out that the man chosen as Hugh's successor, John Sturdy, had commitments which he could not leave until 1965, Geoffrey Lampe should offer to bridge the gap by serving as Acting Dean meanwhile. On Geoffrey's view of the call of duty, however, it was something which one did, and something which he took in his stride. (Perhaps this was why he was endowed by an all-seeing Providence with legs on the longish side.)

A professor at Cambridge has very little real contact with students, and especially undergraduates, at a personal level. In the 1960s, he was actually forbidden to give supervisions (i.e. college tutorials). While, therefore, it was quite a monumental undertaking to agree to have the pastoral care of nearly five hundred students for over a year, I am sure that it was very much *because* he would have this involvement with our junior members that Geoffrey took on the role of Acting Dean. He was ably assisted in this work by a chaplain, Tom Akeley, an American theological student who had just completed a PhD at Pembroke. But it cannot have made the task of either Geoffrey or Tom any easier that they should both take office as 'new boys' on the same day; and the business for both of getting to know the college student community, through small lunch parties and so on, though no doubt one which both Dean and Chaplain found (and made) agreeable, was nevertheless a large additional commitment. But just to show his enormous capacity to serve, Geoffrey took on as well gratuitously the post of Director of Studies of the College's theological students for the same year.

Cambridge colleges, with their tradition of amateur, 'in-house', administration, make many calls on their Fellows to sit on committees, permanent and *ad hoc*; and it would be tedious to list the many instances in which the name of Professor Lampe occurs in this part of the college records. For some, like the Chapel Committee, the Charitable Donations Committee, and the Patronage Committee, he was a natural choice and, given his willingness to be involved, an inevitable one. But in regard to others, such as the Stipends Committee, the committee 'to consider the structure and functions of the bursarship', or the 'Musical Priorities Committee', where the call was surely far beyond that of conscience, he answered it with the same good will and devotedness.

In regard to two or three of these committees, however, a special word is in order. In guiding the electors to the S. A. Cook Bye-Fellowship, he was instrumental in bringing to the college and to Cambridge such distinguished figures as Ernst Bammel, Father James Burtchaell, H. J. Lehmann, William W. Bartley III, Bishop Kenneth Cragg, and M. D. Roaf, and was even able, in these non-discriminatory times, to anticipate the admission of women to Caius by procuring that a lady candidate, Ursula King, should hold her fellowship at Newnham. Then, as Secretary of the Patronage

Committee, as he was continuously from 1963, it was his task to hold the College's hands when making its presentation to the various livings within its gift. Of course this involved the chores of correspondence, arranging interviews, and visits to parishes and so on; but all who were in any way associated with Geoffrey's work in this field pay tribute to the quite remarkable pains he took to find the right man on each occasion. Not every member of this committee fully understood the subtle implications of 'Series Three', or the passions which such issues could arouse in the breasts of churchwardens and parochial church councillors; but Geoffrey was invariably sensitive and sympathetic to such concerns, and worked hard to steer matters to an outcome that was acceptable on all sides.

The other committee which must be mentioned had a brief but very influential and productive life, in the late 1960s and early 1970s. It had no official title but was happily dubbed (I suspect by Joseph Needham, our then Master) '*I Tre Professori*'. To put things into focus, we should remember that this was a period of great, perhaps unprecedented, student unrest, and of change in university affairs across the world. At Cambridge, there was general concern that girl students were outnumbered by men by something like ten to one; but in the traditional male colleges there was great reluctance to do much about the matter. As recently as 1964, the idea that undergraduates might 'occasionally' bring lady guests into Hall dinner was raised as a matter of some novelty; while the notion that Fellows might wish to do the same was still some way off. But by the beginning of 1968, the possibility that Caius might revise its statutes to allow for the admission of women was being actively discussed and, indeed, it was quite widely expected that we might join Churchill, King's, and Clare in the experiment of 'going mixed'. However, a vote taken in March 1969 on the fundamental question failed narrowly to reach the special majority required for constitutional amendments, and so Caius was not in the event one of the pioneering mixed colleges. The immediate aftermath of the vote was, however, unfortunate, in that it left a divided Fellowship with strong feelings running on both sides. The three professors— Charles Brink, Geoffrey Lampe, and Edward Parkes—put together a peace-making and statesmanlike proposal, arguing that Caius should take the initiative in creating further academic opportunities for women at Cambridge, whether or not change was to come at Caius itself. After several terms, during which ideas were mulled over and debated, it seemed that the most likely way forward would be for Caius to find other colleges willing to join with it in launching a new college, to be co-residential and primarily undergraduate. In such a venture, we could draw upon our experience in the foundation, with Trinity and St John's, of Darwin College as a new graduate institution some years before.

At the end of 1971, events took a dramatic new turn, with the appearance upon the scene of an anonymous benefactor, who was looking for a way of giving financial help on a very substantial scale to the university. Ten years later, all has been revealed: the well-wisher was Mr David Robinson, and the outcome of his beneficence is the splendidly-endowed college which he has allowed to bear his name. Although, as things have developed, Robinson College has been established on a basis of autonomy which is greater than we at Caius originally envisaged, and the scale of the new venture no doubt far exceeds the fondest dreams of the three professors who wrote a paper on the topic twelve years ago, it should I think be recorded for posterity that, even before the Robinson benefaction was offered, the initiative to establish just such a new foundation had been taken, within Caius, by Geoffrey Lampe and his two colleagues; and this fact is marked today by a Caian representation upon the board of trustees of the new college.

It would, however, give an altogether false impression to suggest that it was a really significant feature of Geoffrey's time as a Fellow of Caius that he trod its corridors of power and took part in so much committee-work—especially in the case of Geoffrey who, although always willing to serve, was never one to thrust himself forward and was the least officious of men. Much more, for him, Caius was a base for his scholarly work, and a community offering both academic contact and personal companionship into which he could wholeheartedly enter.

He preached regularly in the college chapel, sermons in which he pulled no punches and in which his conviction, his compassion for people, his call for an involvement in the issues of our time and, above all, his integrity as a scholar and as a person always shone through. One or two of his friends treasure in their memories a moment when, at the end of one service, he turned briefly towards the altar and, with that slightly quizzical look over his spectacles that we remember so well, appeared to check that whatever ought to have been present was there in its proper place; then, apparently satisfied that all was well, he turned again to the congregation to give the blessing!

One group which came every year to know Geoffrey especially well and to revel in his company was the college choir. Here, he was able fully to indulge his delight in the company of young people. Former choristers recall vividly their visits to Ely, and the tours which he conducted for their benefit into the higher and remoter parts of the cathedral where the ordinary visitor is never privileged to set foot. His athletic feats at dizzy heights, and the ease with which he manoeuvred his tall (and, in earlier days, not notably slender) frame through narrow openings would, on all accounts, have done credit to his sailor son, and certainly impressed his youthful companions. The choir has, too, a traditional annual tour at the end of June, most often among college livings in East Anglia, but sometimes further afield. Geoffrey, who regularly volunteered to accompany the party and to help as a chauffeur, had an enviable reputation among the boys as a raconteur. There were, too, chapel outings in the summer term, in which Geoffrey and Elizabeth were enthusiastic participants, happy to join in a game of bingo on the coach or to share in a round of iced lollies—or drinks in a pub at the end of the day.

Most memorable of all my own recollections of Geoffrey (and in this one must include Elizabeth as an indispensable partner) is the breadth and openness of their friendship and affection, the warmth of the welcome— as much into their own and their family's lives as into the home itself or the dinner party. Whether the hospitality was in Ely, at the 'Black Hostelry' (where one could enjoy the glimpse through the window of the fruit-cages and the well-tended garden, and wonder how on earth he ever did find time for that as well), or whether—as was more common in later years—they chose to make the College the venue for their parties, there seems to have been no single event in their lives—an engagement, a new grandchild, a ruby wedding—which was not made an occasion for colleagues and friends and their own families to rejoice in and to share with them. This was, perhaps, in older times when fellowship bodies were smaller and families moved about rather less, something that may have been more customary. But for Geoffrey and Elizabeth, this was nothing to do with custom: it was simply a natural thing to extend their family happiness into a wider circle.

For those of us who were privileged to share in this experience, it was something very exceptional.

In view of his eminence as a scholar and of the affection and esteem in which he was held by the Fellowship, he would have been a natural choice as head of the College, had a vacancy come at the right moment. When Joseph Needham left the Lodge in 1975 Geoffrey did, in fact, allow his name to go forward—at a time when he was approaching retirement himself. Knowing, as we do now, how his health was then failing, it was no doubt all for the best that he did not press his candidature past the initial stages: we can only be sure that, had events run otherwise, the talents that both Geoffrey and Elizabeth would have brought to the Lodge were considerable.

On his retirement from the Regius Chair in September 1979, he became a Life Fellow. He continued to be as active as ever in college life until his death a year later, twenty years almost to the day from his admission as a Fellow: the same involvement, the same concern, the same enthusiasm, the same good cheer. And he is still very close to many of us.

'He was a chap people liked', remarked one colleague. But, over and above that, he was a chap who liked people.

THE BOARD OF EXTRA-MURAL STUDIES

by J. M. Y. Andrew, MA

Mr Andrew is President of St Catharine's College, Cambridge, where he has also been Senior Tutor. He matriculated as a mature student in 1947, after having been in the Navy and in the Civil Service. He has spent twenty-seven years on the Board of Extra-mural Studies, ten of them as its Director.

Geoffrey Lampe became a member of the Board of Extra-mural Studies in the academical year 1961–2 shortly after his arrival in Cambridge. It was a happy nomination for the Council of the Senate to make, since he had been chairman of a similar body in Birmingham and therefore enjoyed the distinction, rare among newly appointed university members of the Board, of some familiarity with and practical experience of university extra-mural teaching. This he quickly reinforced, during the Michaelmas Term 1961, by undertaking a course of ten lectures in Wisbech on *Romans*. These lectures were promoted locally by the Council of Churches and were heard by a substantial audience whose enthusiasm had been sharpened in the previous year by Donald MacKinnon. His direct, lucid, and sympathetic exposition assured his popularity in Wisbech, where he was to lecture on a number of subsequent occasions, the most successful of which, at least in terms of the size of his audience and the discussions which the course generated, was that he entitled *Shaping forces in present day religion* and gave in the Michaelmas Term 1966. The distinction of his mind and the gentle and courteous modesty with which he joined his audience in discussion quickly won over Fenland audiences which others had found dour.

The Council of Churches in Letchworth, at the opposite end of the Board's province, learnt of the success of the ventures in Wisbech and invited Geoffrey to lecture to them in the Michaelmas Term 1965. He became warmly attached to this centre and gave a number of courses there which spanned virtually the whole of his tenure as a professor, for he never refused an invitation to give a course of lectures if it was physically possible for him to undertake it. He lectured also in Kings Lynn and St Albans; indeed, the last of his lecture courses for the Board he gave in Kings Lynn to a very large audience in the Lent Term 1977 on *The Bible Today*. These extra-mural expeditions were important occasions in the towns in which he lectured and were very much part of a great tradition of university extension teaching which had started in Cambridge in 1873.

Shortly before he left Cambridge for London, Peter Ackroyd had planned and directed a seven-day residential course on the Old Testament in Madingley Hall, the establishment in which the Board arranged residential courses for a wide diversity of adult students. Well attended, this had identified a need for such courses, particularly among teachers. Geoffrey Lampe decided that a basis existed for further courses aimed at a similar audience and in July 1962 he planned and directed, with the help of Miss O. J. Lace of the William Temple College, Rugby, a seven-day course on *The study of the New Testament*. This was followed by a number of similar ventures at first planned and directed with Miss Lace, later with Miss Jean Holm of Homerton College with whom he first undertook a course in July 1971 entitled *Christian theology in the age of science*. Similar courses are still given, both in the field as university extension lectures and residentially in Madingley Hall: their success derives largely from Geoffrey Lampe's quiet enthusiasm for this kind of activity and from his gifts as a communicator with a large variety of people, many of whom were utterly remote from academic practice.

He became chairman of the Board of Extra-mural Studies in October 1968 and served in that capacity until his retirement. It was an important period in the history of the Board: for example, the substantial and rapidly increasing provision of adult education by Local Education Authorities brought into question, where it did not openly challenge, the nature of the Board's provision, and new patterns of co-operation had to be established which created misgivings in the minds of other partners, for example the Workers' Educational Association; new patterns which were, all too soon, to suffer the effects of severe financial recession. Meanwhile the demand for residential courses had grown and, in 1975, the Board assumed full responsibility for Madingley Hall to which it moved its headquarters from Stuart House in which it had first been established in 1924. To take over a large residential college at this time was not a small undertaking: it was the greatest change in the direction and focus of the Board's work for fifty years. Inevitably, then, this was a period of change and new departures which created some misgivings and no little tension for the staff of the Board, its key committee members and, inevitably, the chairman. It would be difficult to exaggerate the steadying influence or the gifts which Geoffrey Lampe brought to the Board throughout this period. He was very patient and a good listener, dismissive only of specious or dishonest argument; he was a notably courteous chairman of meetings who nevertheless brooked neither ill-humour nor discourtesy and moved the business forward steadily. He had an entertaining talent for failing to hear the irrelevant or merely silly which was perhaps part of his surprising gift, surprising in a man so apparently gentle, for stopping fools in their tracks with little perceptible effort. Because he assumed that men knew their trade, he intervened rarely, interfered never; yet this gave him great influence because he was a man with whom one actively wanted to discuss problems and difficulties, and to whom, as chairman, one welcomed the opportunity to render an account of the Board's progress.

One final virtue should be recorded: his loyalty was of the very highest quality. He made an outstanding contribution to the life and vigour of the university's extra-mural teaching.

AS A CANON OF ELY

by the Right Reverend E. J. K. Roberts, MA,
Hon DD

Bishop Roberts was Vice-Principal of Cuddeson Theological College, Oxford; then held various parochial and administrative offices, chiefly in the diocese of Portsmouth, until he became Bishop Suffragan first of Malmesbury, then of Kensington, and in 1964 Bishop of Ely. He retired in 1977 to the Isle of Wight, where he was at one time Archdeacon. He is now Honorary Assistant Bishop of Portsmouth.

The Black Hostelry at Ely, where Geoffrey Lampe and his family lived from 1960 to 1971, was, as its name suggests, originally part of the complex of buildings of the Benedictine foundation. After the dissolution of the monastery this house became part of the Ely chapter property and the home of one of the residentiary canons of the cathedral.

It was a somewhat daunting task for Geoffrey and Elizabeth to have to make this house which rambles along the south side of Firmary Lane into a real home for themselves and their two children. The Lampe family set to work at once to convert this establishment into a family home, and it was clear from the outset of their time there that Geoffrey had no intention of using the house merely as a *pied-à-terre* for himself, to supplement his college rooms in Cambridge.

Few academics can ever have possessed so many domestic skills as Geoffrey Lampe. He was as handy with a screwdriver and versatile with a paintbrush as he was felicitous with a pen, and as articulate about the plants in his garden as about theological matters in the lecture room. A friend remarked, 'You could never be sure on meeting him, whether he had just come from work on the Patristic Lexicon or whether he had been bottling his gooseberries'. He was as proud of his fruit-cage as he was modest about his scholarship. Ely was familiar enough with scholars. Canons holding Cambridge chairs of divinity had lived for generations in the College. They seemed wise but remote, having little to link them with the local tradespeople and the fenland farmers. But with

Geoffrey Lampe things were immediately different. It was true that the cathedral statutes would have permitted him to count his time in Cambridge as residence in Ely, but he was determined to be both a conscientious professor in the University and also a genuine citizen in the city. Geoffrey often did the shopping with or for his wife; he knew the Ely worthies well, and they greatly appreciated his interest in them and their affairs.

The Black Hostelry was rapidly transformed by the Lampes from being what a neighbour once described as 'an old barn of a place' into an attractive and interesting family home. Downstairs the undercroft was fitted out with a bar and decorated to match this central and unusual feature. Here the Lampes entertained hospitably and imaginatively. There were dinner parties to meet scholars from European and American universities, friends from the town and colleagues from Cambridge; and as often as not there would be a guest in the house in need of a home or a rest. Upstairs in the drawing room, where the southern windows give views over the Dean's Meadow towards Cherry Hill, rising like an inverted pudding basin from its flat surroundings, the Lampes were at home on more formal occasions. But the same warm welcome awaited every visitor to the Black Hostelry, and the family shared their obvious happiness with all their guests and neighbours. One neighbour, especially, benefited greatly from Geoffrey's and Elizabeth's concern. On the opposite side of Firmary Lane from the Black Hostelry is Powcher's Hall. Here during most of Geoffrey's time in Ely lived Bishop Gordon Walsh, who came, after his retirement from Japan, to be assistant bishop and canon residentiary. His wife had recently died, and the bishop, now well on in years, became at once the recipient of the Lampes' affection, and his last years were warmed by his neighbours' generous care.

Geoffrey constantly marvelled at the contrast between life in Birmingham and in Ely. Bizarre was how he described it. These places seemed to have nothing in common but their line of latitude on the map. From a great West Midlands industrial and commercial centre he brought his family to a small East Anglian cathedral city; from a world of fine shops in wide streets, from a busy city surrounded by prosperous suburbs, the Lampes moved to a little market town dominated by a single great mediaeval church that rose out of the fens looking at a distance like some gigantic battleship in stone.

For eleven years Ely cathedral was to be Geoffrey's regular place of worship. The liturgical reforms to which before long the councils of the Church of England were to bend their energies, had as yet not disturbed the old-fashioned high church programme of the cathedral services. Consequently, as he occupied his stall in the choir next the bishop's, he found himself from time to time worshipping in an atmosphere not always congenial to him. But it is a measure of the stature of this man that he never allowed his own preferences and convictions in these matters to diminish his loyalty to the dean or to lessen his appreciation for his colleagues in the chapter. He was punctilious in his cathedral attendances when Cambridge duties permitted, and he took a far larger interest in its affairs than could be remembered of any of his professorial predecessors. He had something important to give to chapter life and he was as generous of his time and abilities as his many other commitments allowed.

When at home he celebrated the Holy Communion each Thursday morning. He followd the Prayer Book order with care, and whenever he deviated from it he was always ready to explain his reasons which were given with assurance and modesty. He wore the eucharistic vestments because that was the practice he found in the cathedral; occasionally they would appear to have been somewhat hastily assumed in the vestry, an outward sign perhaps for Geoffrey of the Church of England's disclaimer that any doctrinal significance attaches to these garments.

Geoffrey was exceptionally good with the cathedral staff and workmen. He knew them and their families well, and they in turn knew they could always obtain a sympathetic hearing and often much practical help from him. He would gladly set to and give a hand with the chores which made up the heavy extra duties of the vergers and bedesmen on big occasions.

Canon Lampe was an obvious choice as chapter librarian and it was largely at his instigation that a major part of the books from the Ely library was rehoused in Cambridge where they would be more readily available to students. His own library became a feature of the Black Hostelry, and as he sat among his books one felt him to be among friends with all of whom he was on familiar terms, and whose contents he was ready to share with every seeker after knowledge who came for guidance.

In the pulpit Geoffrey spoke with the fluency to be expected of an accomplished and experienced lecturer. Sometimes he over-estimated the intellectual reach of the cathedral congregation; he certainly never spoke down to his audience. 'You jolly well have to listen when Canon Lampe preaches', a young chorister remarked. The Ely chapter has comparatively little benefice patronage. However to every appointment Geoffrey brought the considerable experience he gained from the chairmanship of his College Patronage Committee. There are a good many East Anglian parishes in and beyond the Ely diocese that have cause to be grateful to Geoffrey for the meticulous care with which he sought to provide them with their incumbents.

It seemed somehow in keeping with the relaxed and informal family life in the Black Hostelry that when cathedral and university duties were done and the vacation came, Geoffrey and Elizabeth would from time to time set off to far-away places such as the Black Sea ports and the cities along the Danube. Part of the pleasure for Geoffrey of these trips into eastern Europe was that they were unscripted and unplanned. He appeared to his more timorous friends to have an unquestioning faith that everything would work out well, and so it always did.

To live in the College at Ely is to find oneself surrounded by schoolchildren. The King's School, a tenth century Benedictine foundation, now occupies some of the old monastic buildings and other chapter property. The dean is the chairman of the governing body and the chapter provides two of its number to serve as governors, of whom during his time in Ely, Geoffrey was one. He had himself been a schoolmaster and he brought a wealth of wisdom and experience to the counsels of the school. But he was not only a man highly qualified in educational expertise, he was also a priest and pastor, who took a close and constructive interest in the masters, parents, and pupils of the school.

In 1970 Ely had a new dean and the King's School a new headmaster. Geoffrey found time, even though he was himself so soon to be on the move, to guide the affairs of the school at a critical moment in its history. Canon Lampe undertook one further self-imposed duty in his time at Ely. Just outside the College Porta stood the Theological College where Canon Douglas Hill, a chapter colleague of Geoffrey's, had come as principal in 1960. During the years which preceded the closure of the Theological College in 1964 Geoffrey took on a heavy extra burden of lecturing there and gave of his wisdom to the students and made his experience available in full measure to the principal. As is often the case when a man goes the second mile and gives more than duty requires of him, Geoffrey's contribution to the intellectual and spiritual life of the final group of Ely students proved to be a golden act of generosity that those who were privileged to know him must always remember with gratitude.

In spite of all his many preoccupations and responsibilities Canon Lampe was ready whenever possible to help the clergy of the Ely diocese. After a heavy day's teaching and writing in Cambridge he would not infrequently get into his car and drive across the fens to some remote vicarage to address a group of clergy or find his way, sometimes in a thick winter's fog, to a village hall to speak to a deanery gathering.

When arrangements were being made among the East Anglian dioceses to establish a local training scheme for ordination candidates, it was to Geoffrey the bishops mainly looked to help them build academic standards into the course which would allow it to be compared favourably with the established residential theological colleges.

When Geoffrey became Regius Professor and moved to Cambridge, Ely knew that much would inevitably be lost to the cathedral and the city. But his acceptance of an honorary canonry assured his friends of his readiness to preserve his links with the cathedral and the diocese and his desire to respond to the affection and respect in which Ely had come to hold him.

IN GENERAL SYNOD

by Lord Coggan of Canterbury and Sissinghurst

Lord Coggan was Archbishop of Canterbury from 1974–80.
He read Oriental Languages at Cambridge and has kept up
his love of the Hebrew Bible. He was Professor of New
Testament at Wycliffe College, Toronto, Principal of the
London College of Divinity, Bishop of Bradford, and
Archbishop of York, before becoming Primate of all England.
He lives at Sissinghurst, Kent.

*[A correspondent who was once President of the Cambridge Union
speaks of Geoffrey Lampe in Synod as nothing less than a real orator.
Lord Coggan here depicts him in action.]*

Whenever Geoffrey Lampe rose to speak in the General Synod, a
keen sense of interest could be felt among its members. He
generally sat near the back of the hall, but he never had difficulty in
making himself heard. His theological expertise, together with the
fact that he had obviously mastered the details of the subject in
hand, gave an authority to what he said, which was heightened by
his considerable stature and a certain gravity of address which was
not diminished by occasional shafts of humour.

The theologians in the Synod knew, from a reading of his books,
what was the quality of his mind. The others were grateful that one
who was an acknowledged leader in theological matters could
present his case in a manner so devoid of technicalities as to be
easily grasped by an attentive listener. If one's mind was not
already made up, if one was still open to persuasion, few speakers in
the Synod were better equipped than Geoffrey Lampe to win one
over to his point of view.

He built up a case as a builder might erect a wall—layer was
firmly built on layer, a solid foundation having been laid at the
beginning. When he sat down, a wall stood firm which would take
some strength to demolish. Yet there was a courtesy about his
argument which showed that he had little interest merely in scoring
points off those who held an opposite view. *Magna est veritas et*

praevalebit. That he knew, and the knowledge gave him his sureness of touch.

Naturally enough, there were certain causes, certain themes, which were especially close to his heart, and on these he concentrated his thinking and his speaking. We do not find him sharing in debates on finance or on the minutiae of the Legal Fees Order or of the Pastoral (Amendment) Measure. Others with special knowledge of such matters might be left to get on with them. But where matters of deep theological or ecclesiastical moment were concerned, there he could be relied on to intervene with skill and perspicacity. In such a matter as 'The Use of Church Buildings', where questions of theology and of down-to-earth practice were closely intertwined, he was at his best in disentangling the complexities of the situation. In February 1973, he moved 'That the Synod do take note of' the report by a working party (GS135) on the British Council of Churches' Report. He jumped straight into a discussion about the theological concept of holiness—what do we mean if we say that a church is 'God's house'?; what is the bearing on the matter of our belief in God transcendent and God incarnate?, and so on. He even drew on his parochial experience and told, with humour and yet with compassionate understanding, the story of a one-time parishoner of his who was going through a crisis of faith because the gas lighting in their church had been replaced with electricity—the immense brass stand which supported a ring of gas jets had, to her thinking, represented the crown of thorns and had become the focus of her devotion to our Lord's passion. I can hear the Synod laugh, and I doubt not Geoffrey Lampe laughed with them. But he added: 'Whether this means that one should actually apply the concept of holiness to that gas standard I am not sure. Probably one should, for I have no doubt that God made it for her a real means of grace'. I think I could take my perplexities to a man who could look at things in this fashion.

In this same debate, he soon moved on to speak about the difficult question of the handing over to adherents of other faiths church buildings for which Christians have no further need. Arguing that 'the Gospel is not commended by hindering others from practising their religion', he said that he found it very hard to believe that a building that we no longer use is an effective sign of the Lordship of Christ. 'A far better sign that Jesus is our Lord and that the cross is our banner is surely the consideration and care for our fellow men. . . .'

Perhaps we see Geoffrey Lampe at his best in Synod when that body was engaged in debating a subject which, by its very nature, was of a kind which was liable to generate a great deal of heat but not necessarily very much light. Such a subject was the ordination of women to the priesthood. We find him taking part in the debate in November 1972, July 1973, and again in July 1975. Of these three speeches, the first was by far the most important.

There was no doubt as to where he stood in this matter—he was in favour of the ordination of women. Early in his speech he made it clear that the Synod was debating a subject which had been before it for many years. 'The old emotions which used to generate so much heat have now died down and we can look at the question calmly.' He allied himself with one of the opponents of women's ordination in jettisoning 'a lot of rubbish which ought to have been thrown out years ago'—he had no interest in raking over the ashes of issues which ought to be considered dead. What was at issue was *what is good for the Church of Christ in its mission*, not a matter of women's rights. He then proceeded to mention three theological issues which he held should be borne in mind in the course of the debate: The *first* was the relationship between the ministry of the word and the ministry of the sacraments. He found it to be theologically anomalous that women, who now are recognised as having a ministry of the word and a ministry of pastoral care, should be blocked from the presidency of the Eucharist, the authoritative declaration of absolution, and the pronouncement of blessing on the congregation. Must the sex difference 'interpose a wedge between the ministry of the word on the one hand and the ministry of the sacraments on the other?' There was no doubt what his answer was to that question.

The *second* issue had to do with the relationship between vocation to the ministry and baptism into the priestly body of Christ. 'Men and women alike are baptised into the priesthood of which the body of Christ consists as the manifestation of and participation in the eternal priesthood of our Lord.' Men so baptised can find a calling from God to the ministry of word and sacraments. Women are debarred from that twofold ministry. Why? 'There is an increasing number of women today who believe they have actually received the inward call of God to priesthood but

have not received the Church's call to exercise it.' It was clear
that Geoffrey Lampe saw an anomaly here.

The *third* issue was that of complementarity. He was not
opposed to that concept within the ministry of the Church—
complementarity rather than just a reproducing of the ministry of
men. 'There are many jobs that women seem to do better than
men.' That would take working out. But 'it is when you have got
men and women baptised into the one body and ordained to the one
ministry that you can best diversify ministries'.

In the July 1979 session of the General Synod, we find Geoffrey
Lampe making a major speech when there was a debate on the
question of permitting 'women lawfully ordained abroad' to
function as such in England, under certain conditions clearly laid
down. Layer upon layer, he built up his case against those who
propounded the view that no action should be taken. To take no
action, he argued, would be disruptive of the fellowship of the
Anglican Communion; for those who have been legally ordained,
say, in Canada, or in the Church of the United States, or in New
Zealand have been ordained to the office and work of a priest *in the
Church of God.* It would be disruptive of our relations with the Free
Churches. And as for our relations with the Roman Catholics, if
union with Rome is only obtainable at the cost of our impeding
advance on all other ecumenical fronts and disrupting our
fellowship within the Anglican Communion, then the answer must
be 'No'. Lastly, within our own Church of England inaction would
be disruptive. The consciences of those who believe the ordination
of women to be impossible are guarded. If no action is taken, those
who believe visiting women priests to be priests in the same sense
that we are will be compelled to act a lie, and that is an intolerable
position, and one 'which I would ask the Synod not to thrust us
into'.

The Synod was in a cautious mood, and the strong words of the
Professor went unheeded.

Geoffrey Lampe had a mind which could range out into the
future and a belief in the Holy Spirit and his activity in the Church
which forbade him from taking a position of rigidity. This we have
seen in his attitude to the ordination of women. But he could also be
cautious, with a caution born of his knowledge of the history of the
Church and of its errors in the past. Thus we find him, in the
November 1977 session of the Synod, arguing against the

institution of a permanent diaconate. He seemed doubtful as to whether those who were advocating this had fully considered its implications. In ordaining laymen to the diaconate, 'one would make them into clergy, but I believe that in these days we have got to ask very carefully what we mean by clergy. . . . It is quite clear what the priesthood means—priesthood shared by the Bishop and his priests. I am not at all clear beyond that what is meant now by holy orders'. The operative word in that last sentence is 'now'—the modern situation is very different from the mediaeval. Lampe's caution was based on his knowledge of history and his awareness of the contemporary state of flux in our attitude to ministry as a whole.

His caution is seen again in an important speech which he made to Synod in February 1977. It had to do with authority in the Church. The document before Synod was the last of the three 'Agreed Statements' put out by the Anglican-Roman Catholic International Commission and entitled *Authority in the Church—A Statement on the question of authority, its nature, exercise, and implications.* Of Geoffrey Lampe's passionate desire for unity, and not least for unity with the Roman Catholic Church, there can be no doubt at all. Indeed, in this very debate, he said: 'Such unity as we can now enjoy includes, or should include, full mutual two-way inter-communion, not practised just occasionally by individuals, as it is today, but officially sponsored and encouraged by the leadership of both Churches. . . . We here and now have fully enough in common with our Roman Catholic brethren to enable us both together to seek the grace of our Lord in shared communion, to obtain from him the grace of fuller unity . . .' But he was highly critical of some of the conclusions in the Statement. 'What were the Anglican representatives doing?', he asked, when they made the claim that councils are protected from error. 'Did they make no mention of Article XXI?' He accused the members of the Commission of definitely seeming to imply recognition of the authority of the Pope as well as of a council to define dogma. All sections of our Church had protested—rightly protested—when Pius XII defined the dogma of the Assumption *de fide* in 1950. We must not go back on such an attitude. Further, he accused the Commission of leaving undealt with 'a formidable residue of unfinished business'. The matters left there were 'not simply loose ends . . .' but 'largely the nub of the matter of primacy'. He was perfectly satisfied to think of the primacy of Rome in terms of the seniority and prestige of the local Church of Rome, with its historic association with Peter and Paul. But the primacy as set out in the document 'demands a stupendous revolution. . . . It means a dismantling of the curia. It means no more encyclicals like *Humanae vitae* . . .'. And why had there been no mention in the document of principal sees other than that of Rome—'it is very unfortunate that the statement nowhere shows the slightest awareness of the apostolic sees and the patriarchates of the Eastern Churches'.

The criticisms of the document are severe, and I have no doubt that they have been considered with the greatest care by the members of the Commission who have been working over it in detail. By the time this book is printed we shall, no doubt, have seen their reactions to Geoffrey Lampe's speech as well as to the multitude of other criticisms and suggestions which have been sent to the Commission since the document on authority first appeared. Perhaps one may be allowed to add that the passing of time and the accession of Pope John Paul II seem, at least to the present writer, to add point to the seriousness of some of Lampe's remarks.

There were occasions in the life of the General Synod when Geoffrey Lampe felt it to be his duty to hold the Synod back from taking precipitate action. Perhaps that is not the least of the functions of a theologian in a large—and very mixed—ecclesiastical body; for the theologian is able, as others are not, to see where similar action in the past has led to trouble in the Church, and where such action in the present might lead even to disaster in the future. Lampe took a leading part in the debates on Christian initiation which occupied the mind of the Synod in 1974. He made the point that he was 'in no way a fundamentalist for the 1662 Book', but when he saw the Synod considering what he called 'a completely new, non-Prayer Book interpretation of Confirmation', though he had no objection to that *per se*, he felt that the time had come to think much more carefully about it before asking the dioceses to report on it. A brake can delay, even if it does not avert, a disaster! So it was that, when the matter of infant dedication came up for debate, he pointed out that the Ely Commission (of which he had been a member) had made no mention of dedication, nor had the Doctrine Commission's report *Baptism, Thanksgiving and Blessing*. He disliked infant dedication, and he disliked sending to the dioceses for their consideration a matter which had not been properly brought first to the Synod. Once again, Lampe applied the brake. The Synod listened and, this time, were willing to accede to his argument.

Anyone listening to Geoffrey Lampe's speeches must have been aware that they came from a man whose head was well furnished theologically but whose feet were firmly on the ground practically. Towards the end of the debate on Christian initiation, a proposal was made to ask the Presidents of the Synod for another theological report. Lampe would have none of it. 'I hope that for the present we can say "Enough is enough of theological reports on initiation", and try to digest those that we have . . . It takes time for changes in theology to take place. We need to allow an interval for study of these things to be carried on by theologians. Then in a few years time no doubt there will be an opportunity for a further report. . . .' He won his case. The request for yet another theological report was turned down.

Geoffrey Lampe's theological knowledge was seasoned with a down-to-earth realism which was entirely healthy. In a speech on initiation services, he welcomed, *inter alia*, the optional use of oil in Confirmation. But when it came to the suggestion of making the sign of the cross in oil blessed for the purpose, he came down firmly against it. 'This is the oil of exorcism.' The implication of such an anointing is that the candidate for baptism is possessed of the devil, and Lampe would have no truck with such an idea. 'If this is not a matter of exorcism, then it is a meaningless survival. . . . Do not let us clutter our rite with meaningless ancient traditions.' It was a word in season, wisely said.

His down-to-earth realism was seen again in the part he took in the debate on theological training (February 1976). Though, as I have said above, he did not share in debates on general Church finance, in this debate he spoke with serious realism about the increase in University fees and its effect on the theological colleges. 'The theological colleges somehow must shoulder the burden of teaching which has been done by University staffs or pay the Universities on a huge scale to go on doing the job they are now performing.' Fifteen months later, we find him taking up a number of practical points made in a report on theological training issued by the Advisory Council for the Church's Ministry. Perhaps the most important of these points had to do with the length of a man's 'devotional and spiritual education'. He rejected the idea of a two-year theological college course, with one of those two years spent non-residentially, the theology graduate being 'booted out into the world for a year'. He wanted a three-year norm for non-theological graduates, and warned against the policy of cutting down courses. In June 1979, the bishops of the Church of England, the Church in Wales, and the Scottish Episcopal Church wrote to the Secretary of State expressing their 'grave concern' over the likely consequences of the proposal then being put forward to the Government for increases in fees to be imposed on overseas students studying in England and for a significant reduction in their numbers. At the November session of the Synod, Geoffrey Lampe spoke as Chairman of the Higher and Further Education Committee of the Board of Education of the Church of England. He warmly supported the letter of the bishops and also a declaration by the National Union of Students along similar lines. At the end of a closely reasoned argument, he said: 'I believe that the policy being pursued by the Government at the moment . . . is not a shortsighted policy; I think it is a policy that is as blind as a bat. I trust that this Synod will support what the Board of Education and particularly my Committee are trying to do to support the efforts already made to secure a change in this policy'. At the time of writing, no such change has taken place. I venture to prophecy that in coming years our nation will bitterly rue the fact that the Government did not heed the voices of Geoffrey Lampe and others who thought like him.

There was something magisterial about the way in which Geoffrey Lampe made his contribution to the life and work of the General Synod. If that body can, in the coming years, recruit men and women of comparable stature, and if its members can be wise enough to be open to their guidance, we need not greatly fear for the future synodical government of the Church of England.

THE ANGLO-SCANDINAVIAN CONFERENCE

by the Reverend Professor L. Oesterlin, DD

Professor Oesterlin is Professor of Ecumenical Theology and Missions at the University of Lund, and Rector of a parish near the city. He has taken part in the Anglo-Scandinavian Theological Conference since 1959, and for a time was its coordinating secretary.

by the Reverend Canon D. E. R. Isitt, MA

Canon Isitt has worked mainly in and around Cambridge. From 1967–81 he served as secretary, on the English side, of the Anglo-Scandinavian Theological Conference, and helped Geoffrey Lampe in the arrangement of several of its meetings. He is now a Canon of Bristol and Director of the School of Ministry in that diocese.

When the Anglo-Scandinavian Theological Conference met at Lincoln in August 1979, it was to celebrate the fiftieth anniversary of its first meeting at Cambridge in 1929. This jubilee was to have been marked by a visit from the Archbishop of Canterbury, but in the event more exalted duties kept him away, as he had to attend upon the Queen Mother on her installation as Warden of the Cinque Ports. In the chairman's opening remarks Geoffrey Lampe was at pains to explain just what this meant: the Ports were not ports exactly, or not all of them, and the number five must not be taken too literally, and it was of course entirely appropriate that the custodian of these places should be a royal lady seventy-nine years of age, and essential that the Archbishop should be present as she took up her duties. A look of puzzlement settled on the faces of some of those present, as it was meant to. It deepened as the Dean of Lincoln rose to add that this was all doubly deplorable because the Wardenship of the Cinque Ports had in fact been the prerogative of *his* family for some centuries, and it was questionable whether Her Majesty had the right to usurp it.

Such a moment appealed to Lampe immensely. It enabled him to dilate on a complicated area of tradition; it was one of those oddities of life which could be developed into a good anecdote, stored up and polished for the later delight of his friends; and it made an ideal prelude to a week of good company and serious theological reflection.

The history of the Anglo-Scandinavian Theological Conference has been outlined by Ragnar Bring in an appendix to *The Scandinavian Churches*, edited by L. S. Hunter and published in 1965, and subsequently a full account has been circulated in typescript by Bishop Kaare Støylen. Very full accounts of the meetings have been issued regularly since 1929 in *Svensk teologisk kvartalskrift*. The picture which emerges is in some ways a surprising one. In an age of frequent large-scale conferences of an often ephemeral kind here is one which has been in existence for over half a century, which meets only once in two years and which has a membership normally of sixteen to twenty delegates, chosen principally from the ranks of well-known senior theologians but including some younger men and a sprinkling of ecclesiastics from bishops to country parsons. It was to such a small, semi-official gathering that Lampe devoted a great deal of attention over the years, attending its meetings from 1961 and serving as chairman from 1965 to 1979. That he was not alone in attaching importance to this work is made clear by the award to him in 1978 of the Northern Star by the King of Sweden which together with the honorary DD given him by the University of Lund in 1965 was a measure of the important role which Anglo-Scandinavian relations played not only in Lampe's career but in the development of the ecumenical movement over two generations.

In this chapter we shall attempt to show how all this began with an initiative from the Swedish Church, and how the Conference grew from these beginnings to embrace the other Scandinavian countries and to develop its own pattern. We shall then consider Lampe's particular contribution in this field, both through his own scholarship and by the way he selected and shaped the topics which were discussed. Lastly we shall have something to say about the personal qualities which both he and Elizabeth brought to its meetings.

*   *   *

Relations between the Scandinavian Churches and the Church of England form an unusually happy chapter in ecumenical history, and begin almost like a romantic novel in the modern style, in which two people discover how much they have in common with one another and, without the formality of a marriage, establish a long-standing relationship as equal and independent partners. Conversations between the Church of Sweden and the Church of England began officially in 1909, when the prime mover was Nathan Söderblom, then a professor at Uppsala and later Archbishop. In his essay *Canterbury och Uppsala*, written in 1909 and printed in *Svenska kyrkans kropp och själ*, 1916, he describes the event and what lay behind it. There was no wish to make changes or compromises in church doctrine, nor was there any intention of forming a church alliance; rather, as Söderblom put it:

> Here two fully grown Churches meet—not to deny or erase any part of their history or identity (*egendomlighet*), but in order to get to know each other thoroughly and perhaps in this knowledge to find reasons for a continuing trusting relationship beneficial to both. (p. 118)

Söderblom saw how three factors could serve as a basis for closer relations between the two Churches: an unbroken historic episcopacy (on which point he hastened to add that the Swedish Church would never regard this *per se* as a condition for recognising the legitimacy of any Church); continuity in liturgy and tradition; a comparatively large degree of independence from the state combined with a deep-rooted relationship between Church and people. These points of similarity, though expressed for the time being in terms peculiar to Sweden and England, were later to prove useful as a starting-point for the other Scandinavian Churches. In 1909 Söderblom saw them as affording a contribution to the unity of Christianity, and was already making deliberate use of the word 'catholic': Anglican claims in this respect encouraged him in the use of such language even within Lutheran circles.

It is against this wider Anglican-Lutheran background that during the 1920s new understandings developed between the Church of England and the Scandinavian Churches. Theological meetings between English and German scholars had taken place before 1900 without any positive results. Not only had there been national and political tensions on both sides, but the dominating figure of Adolf von Harnack did not prove sympathetic to an English audience. After the Life and Work meeting at Stockholm in 1925 new efforts were made to hold Anglican-Lutheran talks, and Gustav Aulén took part in such a meeting in the Wartburg: but again the results were negative and deep divisions, both national and theological, were evident. So the idea grew that it would be well, for the time being, to encourage contacts between Anglicans and Scandinavian Lutherans, and in 1929 the first Anglo-Scandinavian Theological Conference was held in Cambridge. Once again it was Nathan Söderblom who took the initiative, joined now by Aulén, and at the next meeting at Sparreholm in Sweden by Yngve Brilioth and Anders Nygren.

In the Church of England at this time there was a group of theologians and church leaders whose influence was to be important in the development of these new contacts with Lutheranism: G. E. Newsom, Fellow of Selwyn College, who took the chair at the first two meetings; A. G. Parsons, later Bishop of Southwark; O. C. Quick, Canon of St Paul's; Fr Gabriel Hebert SSM; and during the 1930s A. C. Headlam, Bishop of Gloucester. Other very distinguished names appear in the lists of English participants: Charles Smyth, A. C. Bouquet, Clement Webb, J. K. Mozley, Leonard Hodgson, A. M. Ramsey, W. J. Phythian-Adams, Alan Richardson, L. S. Greenslade, Henry Chadwick, John Tinsley, H. E. W. Turner.

The character of these early meetings has been vividly portrayed by Aulén in his memoir *Från mina 96 år*, published in 1975. Three things are immediately noticeable. First, the question of the historic episcopate was never on the agenda and did not in fact appear to be a subject for discussion: the involvement of the Norwegians and Danes no doubt accounts for this. Secondly, the important thing was to explore common ground in church life generally, rather than emphasise differences. Thirdly, considerable interest was being aroused in England by the emergence in Scandinavia of a fresh theological approach which demonstrated that Lutheranism did not necessarily have to be seen as nationalistic, pietistic, or confessionally oriented. At the 1929 meeting Gustav Aulén presented a first draft of what was to become a widely read study of the Atonement, known in English as *Christus Victor* and published in 1931. At the next meeting Anders Nygren read a paper on Christianity and Platonism which was later to be incorporated into *Agape and Eros*, (English translation, 1953). In Hebert's translation, Brilioth's *Eucharistic Faith and Practice* was by now widely known in English-speaking circles. Hebert also translated a section of Nathan Söderblom's devotional work on the Passion under the title *The Mystery of the Cross*.

So it was that English theologians were encouraged by Söderblom and Brilioth to see Lutheranism in a new light—still deeply rooted in both the New Testament and the early Church, but with a new interest in spirituality and liturgical life. Of equal importance was the discovery that Luther himself, far from being an isolated figure discontinuous with his past, could be seen as a contributor to the continuing life of the catholic Church. It appeared, in the words of one Anglican participant, that 'Luther never was a Lutheran after all'. Nor was it only the Swedish delegates who figured in this new presentation of Lutheranism: Aleksi Lehtonen, later Archbishop of Turku; Jens Nørregaard, Rector Magnificus of the University of Copenhagen; Einar Molland of Oslo University, and on occasions Bishop Eivin Berggrav himself— all represented a fresh Lutheran approach from the point of view of their respective Churches. Over many years the chief spokesmen for this characteristically Scandinavian Lutheranism were Ragnar Bring of Lund and Regin Prenter of Århus, who helped disabuse the English of many misunderstandings of the true nature of the Lutheran tradition, a tradition which has been maintained by a long line of eminent scholars such as Noack, Jervell, Gerhardsson, Lindhardt, Juva, and Herrlin.

What kind of Anglicanism was it that the nordic delegates have encountered during these fifty years? It seemed to the Scandinavians that what was mostly represented was the 'liberal catholic' tradition within the Church of England. Certainly there were seldom to be found at these meetings men of extreme views in any direction, but participants were in fact chosen not as representatives of this or that school of churchmanship: what mattered was a freedom of interchange which was itself both open and radical and which gave full weight to the learned traditions of English Christianity. Particularly attractive to Scandinavians was the style of philosophical theology represented by I. T. Ramsey whose paper at the 1969 meeting entitled *Chalcedon Revisited* is still remembered with awe. And they responded with interest to the kind of theological reflection on Church and Society associated with the leadership of L. S. Hunter and those he brought with him to the conferences of the immediate post-war period. Above all they were impressed by the way these two strands could be combined in Anglican scholarship, and theological insights made relevant to contemporary life without the degeneration of theology into a pseudo-sociological science.

*   *   *

It was into this atmosphere of ecumenical realism and scholarly open-mindedness that Geoffrey Lampe brought his particular skills, taking over the chairmanship of the conference from Bishop Hunter in 1965. His reputation was already considerable, and his intellectual gifts were the more impressive for the relaxed and steady control he exercised over the proceedings, and for the way in which he and Elizabeth gave the feeling of being hosts at a house-party. Birger Gerhardsson comments on this in his In Memoriam notice for *Svensk teologisk kvartalskrift* (57/1981):

> Geoffrey Lampe was a very learned man. His home ground was in patristics, for which there is a distinguished tradition in England, but hardly anywhere in theology or the humanities was he really out of his depth. He moved easily within the great and small questions of exegetical debate, and had a real understanding of current affairs in Church and theology, as well as of the background of such questions in church history, history of doctrine, systematic theology, ethics and practical theology. His openness and breadth lent him a redoubtable skill in debate which he readily deployed both in international ecumenical gatherings and at home in England. We who have been able to share with him in the Anglo-Scandinavian Theological Conferences retain happy and grateful memories of his contributions. . . . His presentation was always relaxed, with the clarity of the real teacher, and an individual approach to the interesting problem. This ease of manner perhaps concealed his assured first-hand knowledge of his extensive and sometimes obscurely inaccessible material. He knew his Church Fathers and had the confidence that comes of working with your own tools.

The question may well be asked why it has seemed desirable to extend this particular exchange between the Church of England

and the Scandinavian Churches over more than fifty years. The
answer perhaps lies in the fact that, by the late 1960s and early
1970s, the seed sown in 1929 was beginning to bear fruit in world-
wide Lutheran/Anglican dialogues. By now the German Churches
were involved, as well as Lutheran and Episcopalian bodies from
America and the Third World. One result of these talks has been
the Pulach Agreement of 1972: another was the setting up in 1979
of the Anglican/Lutheran European Regional Commission.
Amongst those most deeply committed to these talks have been
some who over the years have participated in the Anglo-
Scandinavian Theological Conference.

Another reason for their continuance is to be found in Lampe's
chairmanship, which was particularly valuable in three respects.
He had a great capacity for listening and learning, even when a
point of view differed fundamentally from his own, so that when he
was in charge nobody was allowed to feel excluded from the
processes of free discussion. He had the kind of historical
imagination which was quick to apprehend what the different
Churches held in common in their cultural and spiritual heritage,
and he easily made the kind of connections which enabled people of
different nationalities to feel at home with one another. He was
extremely successful in getting intellectual questions into the
widest possible perspective so that, for instance, the characteristics
of both Anglicanism and Lutheranism were seen not simply in
terms of the sixteenth century Reformation but in the context of
their common roots in the early centuries of the Church. This was
where his patristic knowledge was of great value, and he used it not
in any display of erudition but to rescue both Lutherans and
Anglicans from those habits of thought which had hardened into
pietism and fundamentalism on the one hand, and into party-
centred traditionalism on the other. Partisanship he found hard to
tolerate: it was his many-sidedness which enabled us to see our own
different traditions in a clearer light and a greater depth.

This is not the place for detailed consideration of his patristic
learning; but two passages may be quoted from papers which he
read to the Conference in 1971 and 1975 respectively and which
show that combination of scholarship and familiarity which was
particularly his. In the first he follows a line which was to be further
developed in his Bampton Lectures: the paper is entitled *The Holy
Spirit in the Life of the Early Church*:

The idea of the 'procession' of the Spirit was employed by the Fourth Gospel to illustrate the nature of the Spirit's mission: the coming of the Spirit of truth from God to believers so as to witness to Christ to them and through them to the world. The Cappadocian Fathers and the later creeds transferred the concept of 'procession' from the context of the work of the Spirit to that of his being, and used it to distinguish the mode of the derivation of the Spirit from that of the derivation of the Son. In doing this they were not only giving a misleading interpretation to a scriptural term but building upon it a far heavier structure of metaphysical theology than it could properly support. They thus gave themselves the impossible task of infusing some kind of meaningful content into the purely verbal distinction between the 'procession' of the Holy Spirit and the 'generation' of the Son. Further, the Niceno-Constantinopolitan Creed does not tell us, as we might expect, that the Spirit is of one substance with the Father and the Son, but (again using empirical language) that he is worshipped and glorified with the Father and the Son. The creed, then, which devoted so much attention to the being of the Son says very little about the being of the Spirit. Instead, it speaks rather unsystematically about some aspects of the Spirit's work and the place accorded to the Spirit in Christian worship. The Church, in fact, felt that it could say a good deal, out of the experience of its own life and devotion, about the activity of the Holy Spirit, but found it very difficult, and still continues to find it very difficult, to formulate an ontology of the Spirit parallel to its developed Christology.

The words carry that magisterial, almost governessy tone which comes from deep familiarity with his source material. This familiarity was not simply that of the antiquarian. It was always readily applied to questions immediately facing the Church, as in this extract from the 1975 paper entitled *Salvation in the Pre-Augustinian Fathers*:

Generations of children have sung the words of the old hymn, 'He died that we might be forgiven, He died to make us good, That we might go at last to heaven, Saved by his precious blood'. Few people have asked precisely what these lines mean, even though to a theologian's eye almost every word in them is crammed full of the most profound problems. Most churchgoers are ready to affirm that they have indeed been saved, or will be saved, by Christ's precious blood, although they might find it very hard to say from what they have been saved, or will be saved, and for what or to what end they have been, or will be, saved. Let us, however, try to address questions like these to the early Fathers. The first answer we shall get is that although they are so often content to repeat traditional phraseology taken from scripture, without offering any explanation of it, so that what they say may seem vague and imprecise, they are not simply uttering meaningless religious clichés. On the contrary, beneath all the multiform conventional imagery there lies a deep conviction that the gospel is a true message about man's salvation. So important to them is this truth that it determines the shape of their Christology and so, also, the form in which their doctrine of God, Trinitarian theology, is expressed. Thus, the Nicene faith rested ultimately on the soteriological convictions that it is through Christ that we are saved, and that what we understand by 'being saved' could not be effected by one who was less than God in the fullest possible sense of 'God'. It rested on the application to soteriology of the principle, everywhere accepted as axiomatic though it scarcely seems to be self-evident, that what one receives by participation, or as a gift, and does not possess by nature as an inherent property, cannot be passed on to others. It is sufficient for oneself alone. For this reason, according to Athanasius and the Cappadocians, none but a consubstantial Christ can save; nor can either an Arian Logos or a Macedonian Holy Spirit give life or sanctify.

*   *   *

Patristic scholarship was not new to the Anglo-Scandinavian Theological Conference. Many of the Scandinavian participants were well read in both the Greek and Latin Fathers, and Anglican members had earlier brought their own knowledge with them. And Lampe never appeared simply as a specialist in his own field. Theology to him was invariably an expansive, not a restrictive discipline, and nowhere was this more evident than in the way in

which he chose and elaborated the subjects for the conferences
which he planned, from 1965 onwards:

1965   Baptism
1967   Christian Theology and its Contemporary Setting
1969   Incarnation
1971   The Holy Spirit
1973   Interpretation in an Age of Historical Criticism
1975   Man's Understanding of his Salvation
1977   The Church and the Structures of Society
1979   The Distinctiveness of Christian Revelation
1981   The Future of Western Protestantism

It is instructive to see what Lampe's planning made of some of
these topics. In the late 1960s and early 1970s he was concerned to
call to our attention some of the central doctrinal issues in which
both parties to the debate would from their particular traditions
have a distinctive contribution to make. In approaching a subject
like Incarnation, or The Holy Spirit, a scholar such as Regin
Prenter could be relied upon to speak from a classical Lutheran
standpoint, Lampe himself could contribute his understanding of
the early Church, I. T. Ramsey be brought in to speak as a
philosopher, and local resources tapped, with C. K. Barrett
available in Durham and the Orthodox Archbishop Johannes in
Helsinki. The programmes for these years were, in consequence,
richly varied. For 1973 he turned to questions of interpretation.
Lutherans were vexed by the problem of how their hermeneutical
tradition could avoid erosion at the hands of the historical critics.
Lampe was determined to set the matter in a wider perspective so as
to include the more general issue of how not only scripture but
other important texts, sacred and secular, were to be used and
understood by those who had the task of interpreting them: and so
David Brown was called upon to read a paper about the
interpretation of the sacred texts of Islam. In 1975 Salvation was a
hot topic in World Council of Churches circles: Lampe did not
want to avoid the issue, but he was determined that it should not be
treated either in a narrow 'revivalist' sense or as a catchword for
cultural and political fads and attitudes: so he not only himself
produced the paper quoted above, but also ensured that proper
philosophical attention was paid to Marxist and existentialist
understandings of what salvation might mean.

It is not easy to assess what, in the long term, will be the effect of these discussions on the Churches that have sent representatives to them. It is certain that they have made a deep impression on many individuals who have taken part, and it seems clear that their value has extended well beyond the meetings themselves, as contacts have grown and friendships been established. Indeed, a whole network of reference has grown up: guest lectureships have been arranged, and young priests and theologians have been able to benefit from the warmth of these exchanges. This plainly has been due to Geoffrey and Elizabeth Lampe, who brought to these occasions their own personal style and distinction. The meetings of the Conference have not been lavishly arranged, and in terms of prestige and published material they might seem to be of only minor importance. Yet invitations to attend have seldom been declined. The atmosphere has been easy-going and convivial, the tone of discussion gentlemanly—for some, too much so: there was occasionally a feeling that important differences had been glossed over, but Lampe himself rather enjoyed the moments when argument warmed up, while always demanding courtesy and infusing good humour. Generally the meetings ended with a feeling that important matters had received serious treatment, perhaps in greater depth and with more understanding than if formal expressions of agreement or disagreement had been required of us.

The Lampes were not fond of large-scale international events, but in such smaller gatherings they were at their very best. Elizabeth lost no time in putting visitors at their ease, discovering details about their families, and sweeping them off on shopping expeditions. They were themselves inquisitive and appreciative guests, and would subsequently remember not only the highlights of their visits to Scandinavia but those small details which had been of significance to their hosts. Yet neither of them, apparently, knew a word of any nordic language. Geoffrey, confronted with a language difficulty, would stand quite still, lower his head, and look apprehensively from side to side until somebody came along to interpret and the danger was past; he would thereupon resume the matter in hand, with his particularly attractive smile and some appropriate compliment. He was much given to little speeches of thanks or of welcome and believed, quite wrongly, that Scandinavians expected to be addressed at all times by their full academic or ecclesiastical titles. He gave much attention to the details of hospitality. The day always began with early tea which Geoffrey allotted rather capriciously ('I daresay old so-and-so would rather not be distrubed') in a dressing-gown and with his trousers hitched to a point just below the armpits: some professor or bishop would be enlisted to carry the milk and sugar. And it ended in the pub. His taste in pubs was unpredictable. He might lead us to the saloon of an expensively-restored Georgian hotel. 'Oh yes,' he would say, looking round at the sporting prints and the concealed lighting, 'this is *very* nice.' At Durham, on the other hand, he discovered a local where one could hear a man playing the spoons; and each subsequent evening, if the theological activities looked like going on too long, he would look at his watch and say, 'We ought, perhaps, to begin to draw our proceedings to a close'; and very shortly a small procession was to be seen moving down the street in the wake of a large figure whose pace, though unhurried, was unmistakeably determined.

What remains chiefly in the memory of those who attended the Conference was the rare combination of learning, friendship, and godliness which belonged to Geoffrey Lampe's work as a priest and as a scholar, which gave strength and joy to his marriage, and which made it entirely natural for our activities to combine debate and prayer, eucharist and laughter, in a way which even among theologians is becoming increasingly unusual. How highly this was appreciated may be judged from Birger Gerhardsson's words:

> (Geoffrey Lampe was a deeply devout man, with an inward stamp of truth and maturity. He was an Anglican priest as well as a scholar and an academic. . . . He stood by what he believed, and he did not hide it. . . . He always had plenty to give. In the Anglican Church a visitor can sometimes encounter men who can pass on a wide-ranging spiritual and cultural heritage in which many disparate elements are surprisingly integrated: an acute learning, which preserved an open mind towards other people's tentative opinions; faithfulness to his own traditions, combined with openness to reform; cultural refinement without preciousness; deep seriousness and delicate humour. Geoffrey Lampe was such a man.

7
'HOLY LIVING AND HOLY DYING'

'Since we hope he is gone to God and to rest, it is an ill expression of our love to them that we weep; for that life is not best which is longest, and it shall not be enquired how long they have lived, but how well.'

Jeremy Taylor, *Holy Living and Holy Dying*

'. . . the manner of his dying was as inspiring an example to others as was the manner of his life.'

'We thank God who gave him to us, who sustained him in good times and bad, and who now holds him in light and love beyond this world.—*from letters of sympathy received by Elizabeth Lampe*

The intention was that this book should not be 'hagiographical' and should not present a 'plaster saint'. But it has become harder and harder to resist the impression of sheer saintliness, unassuming—indeed, totally unconscious. The memoir, which could never be complete, would not be even adequate without a section devoted to personal impressions of Geoffrey Lampe's character. In some three hundred letters of sympathy received by his wife, there is an extraordinary unanimity in the descriptions of it. If one writer names his honesty, integrity, charity, and gentleness, another will speak of modesty, gentleness, courage, generosity, wit, and wisdom, and another of his wisdom and courage; yet another of the contentedness of his life and another of his vitality, humility, and kindness: variations on a single theme— to which are frequently added references to his bringing of light. This is not merely a pun on his name; nor does it refer only to intellectual illumination or to a sparkling wit. It is a reflection of a goodness that brought brightness and cheer with it.

His kindness, however, never meant any condoning of insincerity or inefficiency. It has been well said that he preferred dialogue to controversy; but he could display a sort of gleeful pugnacity when the truth demanded it. The Archbishop of Canterbury, in a letter of sympathy to Mrs Lampe, says rightly that he was 'never taken in by the bogus or pretentious'; and Bishop Peter Walker's memorial service address, printed near the end of this section, contains an example of just how devastating he could be as a critic. One correspondent speaks of 'his intolerance of things that were humanly wrong'.

Many speak of his capacity for enjoying whatever good things came his way, whether on a humble or a lavish scale. He emerges from all the incidental remarks as a person of integrity, with no compartment of his life left out. 'His theology', writes one, 'corresponded deeply to his own person.' He represented, says the same writer, 'a Christianity solid and lively, critical yet confident'. 'He had the authority', says a friend, 'of someone who knows the truth about life, the kindness of someone who takes trouble about other people, and the winningness of someone who goes full tilt at life, both in work and pleasure.' 'Geoffrey Lampe', wrote his Swedish academic colleague Birger Gerhardsson (quoted above in Oesterlin and Isitt), 'was a deeply devout man with an inward stamp of truth and maturity. He was an Anglican priest as well as a scholar and an academic.' He possessed, says Gerhardsson, 'cultural refinement without preciousness; deep seriousness and delicate humour'. 'The man and his work were one', says another correspondent; and a Cambridge friend speaks of having 'learned from him as a student, colleague and friend—not only about how to be a theologian, but even more how to be a human being'.

The same impression comes through clearly in these five 'glimpses' contributed by Miss Mollie Batten, OBE, sometime Principal of William Temple College.

FIVE GLIMPSES OF GEOFFREY LAMPE

by Miss M. Batten, OBE

Miss Batten was Principal of William Temple College, then at Rugby, and has been a member of the Anglican Group for the Ordination of Women to the Historic Ministry of the Church, and has played a prominent part in the counsels of the Church.

The first was in the 1930s. The Revd J. O. Cobham was Principal of the Queen's College in Birmingham, then an Anglican theological college. I was Warden at the Birmingham University Settlement. 'Jock' Cobham came to ask me to provide a series of weekly sessions designed to give some critical observation of the social services and local social work; I think this was the first such course at a men's theological college. Geoffrey was among the students in 1936. Although his mind must have been mainly on other things, I remember him as a solemn-faced student who was very appreciative of the part played by the Settlement in the college course.

In my second glimpse the roles are reversed; I was a student, he was a don. He was now Chaplain of St John's College, Oxford; the year was 1949. He announced a course of lectures on the Greek text of St Luke's Gospel. I was at St Anne's College reading for a degree in theology. I had come to Oxford knowing no Greek, but I was learning fast and my tutor advised me to go to these lectures which were given in St John's dining hall between breakfast and lunch, while the sparrows feasted on the left-overs of breakfast amid a faint aroma of bacon. Some of the young men did not think much of the lectures but they were just what I needed.

My third glimpse of Geoffrey is in 1953, when he was the newly appointed Professor of Theology at Birmingham. I was Principal of William Temple College and on our removal to Rugby needed to find a new lecturer in church history; I went to consult Professor Lampe. Not only did he say that he would like to do this himself, but he fell in with my need to fit major turning points in church history into eight lectures in the Michaelmas term to make a course which all our diverse students could attend. He also offered to follow this up in the Lent and Summer terms with lectures covering the syllabus of the Cambridge Certificate in Religious Studies which formed part of the curriculum adopted in the college. So began a period of fourteen years when Geoffrey was almost a weekly visitor, and which lasted well into his career at Ely and Cambridge. He never scamped the work; he corrected essays and took tutorials. He sometimes stayed overnight to take our weekday celebration of Holy Communion. He was a constant, unassuming adviser and friend to many and to me during those long and arduous years. He was always ready with wise and constructive comment however black the situation in Church or State; he had no liking for ecclesiastical gossip. Our friendship flourished for both of us during those vital years.

My fourth glimpse is some years on, when his views on the ordination of women were widely known and he could report with authority on the situation in the Church of Sweden. We were needing a chairman for the Anglican Group for the Ordination of Women, a small body which had been held together for a long time by Margaret Roxburgh, my sister, and me. We thought it would be good to have Geoffrey in the chair as a clergy member of the General Synod. He saw the point and agreed and remained in the chair to steer and advise the Group through the recent harrowing years of disappointment.

My last glimpse was here in Midhurst with his wife Elizabeth in the summer of 1980. They came to stay for a weekend at the end of May. On the Friday evening Geoffrey spoke to a study group who had been meeting in this house through the winter; his address brought light to the darkness through which we had been fumbling. On Saturday we went to Chichester Cathedral to see the Chagall window. He preached in the parish church on Sunday morning— Trinity Sunday. They were about to embark on a holiday which took them to Russia, Hungary, Greece, and Italy. I never saw him after that.

Geoffrey was a great person. Many will pay tribute. I never knew a cross word from him in all the forty years I knew him. He was such a friend. May he rest in peace! One of my lights has gone out, yet it burns brighter.

*   *   *

In 1976 Geoffrey Lampe was discovered, with no preliminary warning, to be suffering from extensive cancer. He entered Papworth Hospital for drastic surgery and for some days he and Elizabeth lived close to the gates of death. But not for a moment did their spirit give in. They infected each other with a buoyant optimism. 'It was in no small measure your devoted love and care', wrote a friend to Elizabeth, 'which kept him going and helped him to do all he did and be all he was.' So together they came through the crisis, and soon Geoffrey, on the way to recovery, was cheerfully agreeing to be transferred to Addenbrooke's Hospital in Cambridge for the inside of a day as a 'specimen' for medical students' examinations. From this he derived plenty of quiet amusement, secretly assessing the candidates and later recounting entertaining gaucheries in bed-side manners. He wrote to The Times *asking whether it was not unusual for a professor to be a question instead of setting questions, and speculating on the problems that might arise for the examiners if a candidate complained that* this *question was unreasonable. As soon as he was discharged from Papworth and had briefly convalesced, he returned with unabated vigour to his duties and pleasures, missing no commitment and refusing no social occasion, and reassuring his shocked and anxious friends by dismissing the whole thing as an unimportant episode. Knowing, however, that every day he lived was now borrowed time, he lived with particular zest and enthusiasm for the next four years. 'His light-hearted disregard of an illness that would have quenched the spirit of most people', wrote a correspondent, 'gave a new brilliance to his personality.' On reaching superannuation from the Regius Chair, he celebrated retirement by a seventy-two mile walk with his son and daughter along the South Downs Way. In July 1980, he and Elizabeth went on one more of their adventurous holiday tours, in Russia and the Balkans, Greece, and Italy: 'we had to; we hadn't been on a proper trip for at least eight years!' They returned in time, characteristically, for them to attend a birthday celebration at which a colleague was being presented with a* Festschrift *(to which Geoffrey had contributed an article); but it was with difficulty that he dragged himself there, looking desperately ill. Shortly afterwards came the return to Papworth. Calmly, he spent the days in hospital ordering his affairs, choosing passages for his memorial services, selecting essays for publication in the collection* Explorations in Theology, *cheering and consoling his family and close friends, and signalling calm contentment even when unable to speak because of the use of a 'ventilator'. His mind was lucid and he was attending to details up to within half an hour of his departure. His surgeon, Mr Terence English, of heart-transplant fame, bears witness to his great courage.*

He died on the Eve of the Feast of the Transfiguration.

There follows what is perhaps, in the end, the most important section of all. It helps to show Geoffrey and Elizabeth together as wonderful parents and as the kind, humane, delightful friends they were to all who knew them. It has been well said that everything was much more 'fun' when they were present: they brought geniality and zest to everything.

It was not for nothing that, to celebrate his 65th birthday, his friends and colleagues presented him not with the customary ponderous volume, a Festschrift, *but with a convivial two-day* Fest: *a thanksgiving Eucharist, at which Geoffrey presided and Canon Purcell preached; a dinner, enjoyed by all; and a prolonged theological debate, at which some of the company read papers analysing or challenging some of his theological positions, and he responded. It was, he said, irresistibly reminiscent of an interminable DPhil viva in which he was the candidate and liable to be failed. But how he enjoyed it!*

More than one observer has acknowledged that the ultimate source of these funds of joy and enjoyment was a deep faith in God. Recognising that good things are given not to be possessively clutched but to be used and used up to God's glory, Geoffrey and Elizabeth enjoyed everything so much because they liberally shared it and let it go. Even life itself, lived with élan and verve, was surrendered when the time came, calmly and contentedly and in the sure and certain hope that it was safe in God's hands and would not be lost.

In what follows, the family have generously allowed their personal memories to be included. Geoffrey was nothing if not a family man, and the picture would be woefully incomplete without their contribution. 'There was such a warmth and love between you', wrote a friend to Elizabeth, 'that it does the world good to hear about it . . . Thank you for caring for him so much that he was able to be so fulfilled.'

But first comes a remarkable statement by a religious who had scarcely met him before his terminal illness, but met him then on so deep a level of prayer that there was instantly a spiritual rapport between them: Mother Mary Clare of the Sisters of the Love of God at Fairacres, Oxford.

A MEMOIR

by Mother Mary Clare, SLG

Mother Mary Clare was Mother General of the Community
of the Sisters of the Love of God from 1954–73 and resides at
the Convent of the Incarnation, Fairacres, Oxford.

I met Geoffrey Lampe on only two occasions. He was a man of great
magnanimity of mind and heart. We were brought together on the
first occasion at the Religious Life Conference of 1974 in York. A
small group of friends met for coffee one evening at St John's
College where the Conference was held, during which the
conversation moved from the convivial to the serious. At the
approach of the small hours Geoffrey turned to me with a clear and
penetrating look in his eye, a look that had already prepared to go
beneath the surface of my answer to his question: 'Reverend
Mother, what is the work of *your* community?' Ruminatively I
responded that our work was prayer, especially the prayer of the
night: that the whole of life became prayer. Geoffrey's look bespoke
his recognition of what I meant. He had not at that time delivered
the Bampton Lectures of 1976, but I found later assurance of our
mutual understanding:

> At a very deep level of human personality God's Spirit
> interacts with the spirit of man in prayer . . . This is made
> possible because the initiative in prayer is taken by God and
> does not depend on human ability and effort. (*God as Spirit*,
> 87 f.)

Our second meeting was in Cambridge at Prospect Cottage, a
place of joy for Elizabeth, his family, and friends. Since our first
meeting Geoffrey had had his first major operation for cancer, and
he had written to me asking for prayer for himself and the needs of
others whom he named. The garden in the paved courtyard behind
the cottage was cool on that hot summer day, the air full of scent of
geranium, sweetpea, and rambler rose. I have a vivid impression of
the purple clematis climbing on the wall. I do not remember what
we talked about: but I remember a deep sense of peace and
acceptance in both Geoffrey and Elizabeth. As we said goodbye,

Geoffrey whispered: 'I rely on your prayers for us'. I told him that I prayed for them both each night.

Two meetings, and two more letters afterwards to report progress: and then the last letter, full of confidence as he faced the reality of his death. One sentence stands out in my mind: 'My illness has taught me more than any theological exploration: it has taught me of the reality of God's love and the sustaining power of prayer'.

I am humbled by the way in which God brings love and understanding out of suffering, that friendship can grow through prayer, even with very little meeting. Geoffrey died in the knowledge that all relationships which God gives to us are a blessing and a mystery.

[The following poem was shown to Geoffrey the day before he died by Bishop P. K. Walker who, because of Geoffrey's appreciation of it, quoted it at the marriage of Celia Lampe to Clive Thorp in Ely Cathedral, 13 September 1980.]

I offer you my love, my life and death,
The whole of me. I have no more to give;
And life, alas! is brief and fugitive,
And Death the passing of a moment's breath
And both are far too frail (the mocker saith)
To wake the poet's song or stir his dreams;
For Life and Death are shadows, as it seems
From some dark world which none remembereth.

Yet is there one bright star which shines above
All darkness and all gloom, all change, all strife,
That builds of mortal dreams immortal truth,
That keeps for ever young the heart of youth,
That is the death of death, the life of life,
The star of stars, my star, whose name is Love.

Bishop George Bell

FROM THE FAMILY

'PA'

by Celia

Professor Lampe's daughter Celia spent a year in France after leaving school. She trained as a bilingual secretary in London and then spent two years in Vienna working for the United Nations Industrial Development Organisation. From 1973 until her marriage in September 1980 to Clive Thorp, a New Zealander, she worked as a freelance conference secretary for the United Nations in Geneva, studying music in her spare time. She is now living in Wellington, New Zealand and working for a degree at Victoria University.

Where should I begin? There are photos of Pa and me frozen in a moment among bluebells in a wood near Oxford, or on a beach during one of the few hot English summers where the camera is focused on me, about two years old and hidden by a large sun bonnet, but I am framed on my right by two long legs and I am holding onto an arm which disappears into the picture frame. Of these times I have no real recollection, which is a pity. I think my first vague memories cannot, however, have been much later in life. I was often carried on Pa's shoulders and clasped my arms around his head. How different the world looked—how vast! It was very much like having a ride on some huge animal. I remember measuring what seemed like an eternity between each stride and marvelled at the ground that could be covered in such a way. At the end of the ride he would draw up alongside some bank and I would be gently unloaded.

I soon realised that Pa was not like anyone else's father. At school I listened open-mouthed to tales of the ways my friends were punished by their fathers—their treats and outings were curtailed and they were shouted at and spanked. One was even locked in a cupboard. Of course all this made me wonder when I visited their houses for tea and was welcomed by a smiling father, but I believed them and did not smile back. My father was extraordinarily gentle and I never heard a cross word from him. He was always smiling and full of encouragement. However, this encouragement took a slightly unusual form which I was not to understand fully until later on.

I began to realise that my father wanted me to be happy, and nothing else seemed to matter. I was not encouraged to be top of the form, or even bribed to do so as were some of my school friends, and he did not care a hoot whether I was in the school team. Rather, when I came racing across the Dean's Field in Ely on the back of a fat Welsh cob, I was greeted by his laughter, and a remark which I was to hear very often, 'That's nice Mousy', and he seemed perfectly happy. Laughter was one of the most important things. It meant the happiness he wanted for my brother and me. We always had such fun. My mother dreamt up a lilac and yellow gypsy caravan for us in Wales, and my father, a horse to get it there. My mother found us a pony trap and painted its high wheels, which the long-suffering horse had to pull round the fens. My father took us out on 'reconnaissance trips' before we set off on long trips into Suffolk, to make sure we knew where we were going, or rather, I have the feeling, to show us what beautiful country he had chosen for us although of course he did not say so, and included in this information of a very special nature on how to cross the A10 in this pony trap on a public holiday, or which bridge to take over the M1. We had magical houses, again my mother's creation, with huge playrooms and Norman arches lit up, their dog-tooth pattern matching the zig-zag of a Picasso painting hung on the wall next to them. Tremendous tea parties were given for our friends, pantomime outings *en groupe* were arranged, firework parties where once, to our delight, the box of rockets caught fire and we all watched a magnificent display which lasted a full three minutes.

We went up mountains with my father, and on ships to Scandinavia for the Anglo-Scandinavian Conferences. During winters at Ely he took us skating, and my brother and I would swoop around him on a frozen fen with ducks flying overhead. I would delight in taking Pa over to look at a spot where the ice groaned and sagged as the fenmen raced over it. He would raise his hands and jump around in mock horror. I like to think that he and I had the same sense of humour. Many's the time we hooted with laughter at the same things, and it was a joy to listen to him telling a Groucho Marx joke when he took the part of the snooty New York hostess and would lean forward to give Groucho's wisecrack reply. There are so many happy memories that it is difficult to pick out a few, but I never tired of hearing his version of how the lazy Welsh cob heaved itself over a course of jumps at a show, looking as totally fed up with the whole thing as I was to be on its back, and how it finally managed a nonchalant clear round disregarding the judges who had long stopped using their watches to time us.

However, these incidents were but one aspect of having such a wonderful father, and there are more important things to say. I was totally trusted and allowed complete freedom to choose my own path through life. My efforts landed me in some sticky situations. Sometimes I came home disillusioned with my choice, and yet I had always been given gentle encouragement to go ahead (I nearly said 'to try it out', but this was not the case). When things did go wrong there would be a special tea party. My father, mother, and I would sit round, hold hands, and I would blurt out my woes. When I had done so and was able to decide on a course of action to remedy the situation, encouraged to do so by a hand from each parent, he would say: 'Well, I think that's a *very* good idea', and I would set out again. Fortunately these tea parties took place at less frequent intervals as time went on. Occasionally I was able to provide *him* with an enjoyable time. When a portrait of me was in a big exhibition in Basel, Pa got on a plane at very short notice and came to see it. We drove from Geneva where I was living at the time up into the hills of the Jura where we visited the artist's family, amidst a lot of French shrugging and raising of eyebrows, and we drove on to Basel in a snow storm to visit the exhibition. I still think the best part of the week-end was sitting in Basel's most splendid cake shop, where we imitated the other customers and offered each other cake in very aristocratic German. But here, again, I keep returning to those special times.

I like to believe, selfishly, that he and I had a special relationship—one of complete understanding—but then he had such relationships with everyone with whom he came into contact. However, I feel that over the last few years our understanding became very strong. His preparation for death was a strong confirmation of his life, and his attitude to my brother and me was what it had always been. It was a time, above all, when I felt more privileged than ever to have this person as my father, and I found it difficult to be sad in the face of such utter peace. As I said earlier, there was a disparity between what a father was and what he was. Here, again, I felt that there was a contradiction in what death was supposed to be and what he was making it become, with a total absence of the 'stages of death' that I am now being taught about at university—but this was then a final lesson to his children and the end of an exemplary life. Our 'understanding' carried me through a very happy wedding to Clive only a few weeks later, which was what he had wanted. Then, as now, it was as if, as in that early photograph, he was giving me continued happiness while remaining just out of the picture.

'LOVE, JOY, PEACE'

by Elizabeth

Enid Elizabeth Roberts married Geoffrey Lampe in 1938,
and was his partner in all his activities, devoting her artistic
and social gifts to their home.

*[Letter from Elizabeth Lampe to her daughter Celia, in Wellington,
New Zealand, Autumn 1981]*

My dearest Celia,

Now that more than a year has gone by, I find I can write to you
about your father.

It is hard to believe a year has really gone. Cambridge, the river,
the trees, are still there, but none of them will ever look quite as they
did. I look at the trees as I walk across Christ's Pieces, at their
yellow autumn leaves, and can't really yet believe that he and I will
never walk there and look at them again together; and yet the
darkness and loss are beginning to go, because I'm beginning to
know with increasing certainty that part of him is still with us. I
only know it sometimes—when I listen to very beautiful music in
Caius chapel, or sometimes at Communion, when I know quite
unmistakably that he is there.

So I can write to you about him at last, with love and gratitude.
He gave me so much; such a wonderful life, and he left me such
lovely things to help me to get along—you, Nick, the family, the
continuing prayer and marvellous help I have also had and still
have. So it is possible to put down something of what he meant to
me, beginning with the first sight of each other, when he seemed to
like what he saw, a young girl of eighteen coming down a hill in
Devon, long ago.

After that, we were together in a way so complete it is hard to
define. Perhaps because we were young and I came of a liberal-
minded family we thought alike on many things. His basic
theology, always progressive and liberal, I could understand,
because we were on the same wavelength about that and everything
else, race, politics, everything of real importance. And luckily I had
enough sense to realize I had married a scholar and he needed
someone who would make sure he had peace and quiet when he

needed it, who never expected him home 'on the dot', cared passionately about his views and supported him in every one of them and, most important, someone with whom he could truly relax and enjoy life. A sense of humour made this part of it extra care-free and joyous.

On a deeper level, getting to know the man I had married was like slowly learning to hear a great piece of music. At first it only appeared to be happy and serene; later I began to hear its depth and power, and, at last, the great central theme—profound and holy, the spirit of God in which he lived, and I did hear it, though it took me half my life to do it. Looking back at life together is like looking back at a wide panoramic view of a still, sunlit landscape. Storms and clouds passed over it and were gone and forgotten, because it was always lit by his own basic happiness and love for us.

Death could not separate us from him. I know that increasingly, as life begins to come back into perspective. Because he is part of God's spirit his own serenity comes through more and more, and his light shines more easily through the slight barrier of death. Because he was always so much a part of God, he comes back into our lives very easily, as easily as he left us in the summer afternoon at Papworth, content, confident, and at peace.

Someone else, using the imagery of another century describes it. He left us to go '. . . into the house and gate of Heaven, to enter that gate and dwell in that house where there is no darkness nor dazzling but one equal light, no noise nor silence but one equal music; no ends nor beginnings but one equal eternity; in the habitations of Thy glory and dominion'.

Love, joy, peace, are words your father often used and are what that prayer is all about, and though he lives in that love and joy and peace, he shares it with us and includes us in it in his love. So at last I am learning to be glad, to put aside the grief and welcome him with joy.

'THE TWINKLE AND THE SMILE'

by Nicolas

Nicolas Lampe was born 10 December 1946. Educated at The
Nautical College, Pangbourne, he served his Apprenticeship
as Navigating Cadet with P & O lines and obtained his
Second Mate's Certificate in 1968. He served as a junior
officer with P & O, and qualified as Master Mariner in 1974.
After a few years with Overseas Containers Ltd he left the sea
and now works as Container Controller for the Australia New
Zealand Europe Container Service Executive. In 1971 he
married an Australian, Anne Barbour, and they have two
young sons.

It is almost a year since my father died and writing down my
thoughts and memories of him is, of course, an emotional
experience bringing back the sadness of parting mixed with the
happiness of past shared experiences.

A very good friend of mine, a fellow seafarer, described to my
mother how he remembered the welcome my father gave him. As he
approached and was recognised by my father there came 'first the
twinkle and then the smile'. It is that twinkle and smile I too
remember best of all.

In describing what he meant to me as a father, it would be easy to
indulge in hyperbole. Others can judge dispassionately his
scholastic achievements, his public life. Every father-to-son
relationship is uniquely private and it would be presumptious to
claim that I deserved more sympathy for his loss than others.
Nevertheless, to me he was the perfect father. I have often thought
that perhaps the fact that he could not remember his own father led
him, as a child, to think of what an ideal father should be like and
that later he was able to live up to this standard. Certainly for those
thirty-four years I knew him he was always understanding,
forgiving, 'slow to anger and of great kindness'. Almost his
strongest rebuke was a despairing cry of 'For Pete's sake, pipe down
you two!'. It is easy to remember his quiet disappointment at our
failures and the excited twinkling of his eyes at our successes.

Although my father's work often restricted the amount of time
he could spend with us, there are so many happy memories that it is
hard to know where to start. My earliest memories are of Oxford,

where I can so clearly remember the way he held my hand as we crossed St Giles' to the little sweet shop where he would buy me a sugar mouse before taking me on the bus to kindergarten. Once or twice in snowy weather he would pull me there on a sledge he had constructed out of the remains of Celia's high chair.

One of the most exciting events for a child in Oxford was the annual St Giles' Fair, held immediately outside our house. The best part was sharing a mat with my father as we slid down round and round the helter-skelter. Then at night, sleep being impossible, Celia and I would sit up on the window seat he had built in the bow window of our upstairs nursery and watch the huge moving crowds of people, the twirling coloured lights and spinning roundabouts, and listen to the jolly tunes thumping out of the fairground organs.

Other early delight were picnics in Bagley Wood surrounded by bluebells, or by the river bank at Old Marston. Looking back over the years these were only the first of the many fascinating places my father was to take me to.

The caravans at Aberdaron provided us with wonderful childhood holidays for nearly seven years, all of which recall many images of my father—cooking up the bacon he called 'Pop-pop's frizzly', sitting on the cliffs overlooking Bardsey Island and pointing out to us the diving cormorants, pursuing fish through the shallows and rock pools of the seashore, and his strong arms pulling us across the bay in a rowing boat.

The careful thought and determination with which my father provided such a delightful holiday home for us was a prime example of how he could always see that with imagination, and despite limited resources, it was possible to make things that much more interesting and enjoyable for those who were with him. My mother always claimed that the walk might be long, the climb seem daunting, the temperature chilling, but the objective—perhaps a stunningly beautiful view or an architectural gem—was invariably worth it.

My father always enjoyed long walks and every year he and I would make an assault on the summit of Snowdon; over the years we scrambled up each of the recognised tracks. The first time he carried me on his broad shoulders for a good part of the way; the last time we both climbed over the three peaks of the 'horseshoe'.

A few years later the two of us spent a marvellous week walking in the Italian Alps around the Aosta valley. My father always set a cracking pace, determined to reach his objective. Apart from the spectacular alpine scenery we also explored the mediaeval castles and Roman archeology of the region. As always he seemed to have an amazing knowledge about his surroundings, indeed everywhere we went to he was the only guide I ever needed.

Christmas was always a wonderful experience in our family, and even in recent years it never lost the magic of childhood. Always this magical touch was provided by father. Wherever we lived, certain things never changed. First my father would take Celia and me out foraging in the countryside for holly and fir to decorate the house. In Birmingham on Christmas Eve, he and I would carry an enormous Christmas tree home from the Bull Ring. The decorations went up on Christmas Eve and stayed in place until Twelfth Night. With great care my father would make a wreath of holly for the front door, and when we were asleep he would place holly over every picture frame and hang a bunch of mistletoe in the hall. At our lovely home at Ely he spent hours stringing together long garlands of greenery which he hung up and down the arches of the undercroft.

After all the preparations there were lovely church services to go to—the warmth and sparkle of carols at St Martin's in the Bull Ring, the magic of the candlelit procession to the crib at Ely Cathedral, the supernatural beauty of Christmas Day evensong at King's College and the joyful midnight Communion at Thaxted.

Back at home, my father would preside over a superb Christmas dinner, carefully carving the goose and igniting the pudding. Afterwards he had a look of child-like delight as he distributed all the presents, watching with eager anticipation as we opened the gifts he had so thoughfully wrapped for us. Then the highlight of the day as we sat down to tea and father lit all the candles on the tree.

On Boxing Day my parents threw a party for all their friends. I can see my father now ladling out glasses of steaming hot punch as the room filled up with more and more people, and the chatter and the laughter increased to a crescendo, with his own distinctive laugh often audible above the hubbub. At the end of the party he would invite the 'survivors' to sit down around the fire while more delightful stories were told.

Such were the occasions that I recall when I think about him, but the memory of him is much more than can be linked to specific occasions. He had a clear insight into my own character and understood what kind of life would make me happy. If he ever harboured ambitions for me to follow in his academic footsteps, he kept such thoughts strictly to himself. When I decided that I wanted to become a mariner he gave me every possible encouragement and practical help and advice, and rejoiced when my hopes were fulfilled. Other things too he gave me; his love of fine music, his appreciation of art, his enjoyment of travel, and he tried, by his example, to show how to live life to the full with calm deliberation and an understanding of other people's circumstances and view points, even if he politely disagreed with them.

In later years I loved him above all for the way he welcomed my wife, Anne, so that they came to love each other almost like father and daughter. More recently came the happy day when he cradled his first grandson, Stefan, in his arms. On a warm spring morning, just after completing a course of radiotherapy, he baptised Stefan in Balsham Church.

Some eighteen months later he was off once more on a great walk along the South Downs Way. His tall figure, with a knapsack on his back and his walking stick jauntily striking the ground, strode across the high, open skyline while Celia and I struggled along behind, and it seemed for a while as if the pain and sickness of the past few years had been completely forgotten.

Just before another joyous Christmas his second grandson, Gavin, was born. The following summer, on a beautiful July day, he baptised Gavin with great love and tenderness, but by then he was very ill.

Almost exactly a month after Gavin's Christening the end came at Papworth Hospital. Even during his last days he could make funny faces at his little grandsons so that he was still surrounded by joy and laughter. In the end he showed me that death, as well as life, could be full of love and beauty, and no father could do more for his son than that.

MEMORIAL ADDRESSES

There follow two memorial addresses (with thanks to the Bishop of Ely for permission to print) and, finally, the very remarkable sermon on death by Geoffrey Lampe himself. John Mere, one time Registrary of the University of Cambridge, who died on 13 April 1558, left an endowment for a University Sermon to be preached in St Bene't's Church on the first day of the Easter Term each year. He left quaint instructions as to the choice of themes. One of these, seldom chosen by preachers in more recent times, is the preparation for death. It was chosen by Geoffrey when he was the Preacher on 15 April 1980, four months before his own death.

AN ADDRESS AT A PRIVATE THANKSGIVING EUCHARIST

[in the Chapel of Gonville and Caius College on 9 August 1980]

by Professor the Reverend Canon C. F. D. Moule, Hon. DD, FBA

Professor Moule was for many years Lady Margaret's Professor of Divinity at Cambridge. He is a Fellow of Clare College and an Honorary Fellow of Emmanuel College. He is living in retirement in Sussex.

Having been given the wonderful privilege of saying something now, I have naturally enough asked myself what to choose out of all the beautiful things that might be said. I will say just this: I have sometimes attempted to preach about what is called 'detachment'. But whereas I think about detachment and preach about it, Geoffrey lived it and showed it to us.

By 'detachment' is meant, of course, not a detached indifference to the good things of life, but the very reverse. It means the ability to enjoy life to the full and to affirm material goods positively, precisely because they are not possessively clung to but used—and used up—in an open-handed, generous way.

To see this, as we have seen it in Geoffrey and Elizabeth and their family (I am allowed to say this because, in your kindness, you have invited in one who can speak objectively as an observer, from just outside)—to see this is one of the most lovely things imaginable.

They have entered with zest and enthusiasm into the good things and the good occasions of life, and made everything such fun for everyone else, precisely because they have always been ready to part with them, pouring out their time and talents and possessions in an unanxious, unpossessive way, and just as ready to fling them all away and share pain and privation with others.

This most lovely, most beautiful detachment is a rare jewel, and I don't pretend that I possess it yet. And I ask myself how it is achieved—this glorious freedom, this sort of serious, deep, sympathetic light-heartedness.

Perhaps Geoffrey has given us a glimpse of the secret by his own unerring choice of these readings. Wisdom, Romans, St John—all three of them are about belonging to God:

> . . . the souls of the righteous are in the hand of God . . . he watches over his holy ones.

> Who shall separate us from the love of Christ? . . . not death nor life nor anything else in all creation.

> . . . this is the will of him who sent me, that I should lose nothing of all that he has given me, but raise it up on the last day.

Geoffrey was convinced that he couldn't fall out of God's hand: he was safe—safe under that terrible hail of missiles in the war, safe when he and Elizabeth and the family walked together in the dark valley of death. Whatever happened, he knew he was safe—not in the timid, protective sense, as though one were in a castle (which is never safe, because it can be stormed), but safe in the joyful freedom of one who has faced facts with Christ, and knows that he 'belongs'.

That, I believe, is the secret of his ability to live largely, generously, unanxiously; and to die (as that beautiful notice put it) 'content and in total peace'. It was because, having God, he had all, and, held by God, he knew what real security means.

After such keen enjoyment, to see him no longer is an indescribable privation. Yet, in the pain, we know that they still possess one another in the only ultimate sense of possessing.

And this is the reality that God offers us all. I believe this, though I am still so far from it myself. He offers it to us, patiently and over and over again. He offers it to us now, in this Eucharist. For as often as we eat this bread and drink this cup—guests graciously welcomed to the Lord's High Feast—we declare the Lord's utter aliveness through his own total self-giving. We gratefully acknowledge as Master and Lord the one who used life up into life eternal, and who beckons us to follow him.

AN ADDRESS AT THE MEMORIAL SERVICE

[in Great St Mary's Church, Cambridge, on 18 October 1980]

by the Right Reverend P. K. Walker, MA, Hon. DD

Bishop Walker took a first class in Lit. Hum. at Queen's College, Oxford, after war service with the Royal Navy, was a master at Merchant Taylors' School, Dean and Fellow of Corpus Christi College, Cambridge, and principal of Westcott House. He was then made Bishop of Dorchester in the diocese of Oxford, and from there came to be Bishop of Ely in succession to Bishop E. J. K. Roberts.

1 Peter 4.19: Let them . . . commit the keeping of their souls to God in well doing, as unto a faithful Creator.

So Geoffrey Lampe died, and all his own clearsightedness was with him to the end.

Some words come back to me from near the end of the great last book he left us, *God as Spirit* (p. 204).

'God as Spirit creates Christlikeness. It is in the light of this that we must understand the Johannine sayings that the work of the Spirit of truth is to guide us into all the truth, and that Christ is himself the truth. The guidance of the Spirit is to lead us into Christlikeness, to communicate a deepening understanding of the nature of love. If, then, we pray in the words of the ancient collect to be granted by the Spirit "to have a right judgement in all things", this will mean an ethically right judgement, a view of all things in the perspective of unselfish and Christ-like love'.

'To see the world and ourselves clearly and steadily within that perspective' (of love, that is to say)—that would be the final measure of our response (again so much Geoffrey's word, and for him our own responsiveness was itself something always *given* to us) to the Spirit's guidance.

He was a large man. It is the largeness of his perspective which one remembers: and the clearness and the steadiness of his gaze. We have all been at the receiving end of that look of his—particularly perhaps as he was listening to what it was that we were trying to say. And more often than not he would have picked out of what you had said something that he could give his familiar nod, his own distinctive yes, to, before he then somehow placed it, and you with it, in the larger frame of reference which was his own.

Outreach was another favourite word. God's outreach to us, his continuous outreach, was a constant and a central theme—with what some would say was a naughty impatience with the question was he using words metaphorically or analogically. Which was it? Never mind. God reaches out to us. He listened once as I read out to him a fragment of a review of the autobiography of an Indian Civil Servant. 'X is a man of atonement,' the reviewer had concluded, 'always groping for better meanings.' But groping is not quite the word for Geoffrey—his vision was too clear. Reaching out, say rather—and, because of course the truth was what it was all about, reaching out for better meanings. And 'better meanings' would imply the primacy somehow of the unitive: he was a man of atonement, love having the secret, Christ being himself the truth.

I have a fear that at this point the feet are in danger of leaving the ground. That would not be a worthy remembrance of Geoffrey—of Geoffrey whose first front-line book, *The Seal of the Spirit*, that classical examination of the fathers and doctors of the Church on Christian Baptism and Confirmation, was prompted in fact by his experience as a chaplain in the war-time citizen army as he was pleased to call it. They were days he was ready sometimes to recall, with no false nostalgia and yet with the real remembrance that for a time we had known a society that was co-operative rather than competitive, and he is remembered still by the men whose lives he shared. He had been concerned to explain to one of them—so he recalled in later days to Gordon Kendal—why the Church at home was fussing about instruction before his child could be received: and then, more severely—and one could think of this as going very deep, for he was man of particular tenderness towards children—he had been concerned to come to terms with why the Church had dealt as it had done with another such a soldier's family—to the point of having seemed to deny the thing that it was all about: the outreach of God's love. Where did the truth lie?

Securus iudicat orbis terrarum . . . If Newman found assurance once in invoking the judgement of history, Geoffrey seemed almost sometimes content to rest himself upon the judgement of the ordinary man. He was concerned for the generality, he reached out to him; he went out across the fens of winter's evenings to share his understanding with some extension meeting; his membership for twenty-five years and later chairmanship of the Board of Extra-mural Studies was both real and in its very name symbolic; and in the week of his death no less than three letters to his Bishop lamented the loss of him after one meeting from the new Standing Conference on Religious Syllabus in Schools. In the judgement of the ordinary man, however gropingly, charity *was* what in the end it was all about. And so, returning in his swan-song to his earlier theme, he could write, on the requiring of evidence of commitment from those seeking baptism for their children, 'The most searching test, in any case, is probably that which the Christian community, represented by the local congregation, ought to apply to itself: can it undertake to care for new members, children especially, in such a way as to communicate the Christ-Spirit to them, and is it a recognizably Spirit-inspired body? Is it, in other words, worth joining' (*God as Spirit*, p. 192.)

But I have another fear at this point, and it is that what I will have said will have seemed to miss the *importance* of Geoffrey: his importance in his pure field, as a theologian, as a doctor of the science of GOD. And I am thinking here not simply of his massive erudition as Editor of the Patristic Greek Lexicon, nor am I thinking of my own naughty enjoyment, as late as last May, of the professional at work in a review (an enjoyment, one might confess, of the same order as reading A. E. Housman in the footnotes to his Lucan): 'Where so much appears at first sight to be nonsense it scarcely matters that on p. 28 a misprint occurs in a Latin citation and the translation of it is a shambles, "Gallius" appears for "Gellius" on p. 89, *ecclesia semper reformanda* is said on p. 121 to mean "the church reforming itself", and on p. 5 we have the now almost universal "supercede". What can be recommended to students is the full bibliography, English and German'.

It should perhaps be added that the book in question was one by a continental scholar. Geoffrey was at home on the continent of Europe: one had only to see him moving with his natural and easy authority with Edward Schillebeeckx and other such pioneering men, at a Conference in Nijmegen in the 1960s to see that;* and his Anglo-Scandinavian Conferences, pioneered with friends like

---

* For the papers of this Conference, on Secularization, in 1967, see *Theology* (ed. G. R. Dunstan) February 1968 and following, with G.W.H.L.'s paper 'Secularization in the New Testament and the Early Church', in the April number (163–75).

Gustaf Aulén and recognised when the King of Sweden made him a Commander of the Northern Star, show indeed a perspective that was European. And he worked through personal friendship, personal hospitality, in scholarship as in church relationships. Yet he remained, I think, essentially English in his thinking: and there was a style of continental theologising (do we call it still 'crisis theology'?) which was just not Geoffrey's cup of tea.

But, to leave Gallius to his fate, and to think of Geoffrey as Doctor of Divinity concerned with the reality of God: it was as such that he commanded the stature that he did among us when he had words to say in the General Synod, as University member ('characteristically on guard', as David Jenkins wrote of him once, 'at the intersection of theology and practical affairs'), about practical/pastoral theology, about the Church's ministry, the nature of it and its ordering, the ordination of women to the historic ministry of the Church (to which he was committed), the working together of the churches (for which he passionately cared, and showed his care for it in his concern for the Cambridge Federation of Theological Colleges), yes, and their stance towards the world: he addressed himself to these questions, and he addressed us on them, in the dimension, always and no less, of his own understanding of GOD.

His importance in his pure field as a theologian was precisely the primacy that he gave to GOD: a priority so absolute that nothing must compromise it. And if this God had, as he believed, acted decisively in Jesus to convey to us the great transforming and redemptive disclosure of his judgement, compassion and love, then, try as we must to articulate our understanding of the richness of GOD's being, we must be ready to acknowledge the limitations of our human grasp of it. We must be ready to reappraise as in other fields of thought our frames of reference, our categories, even the 'given' language of the 'persons' within the Godhead—there one saw his intellectual courage, and it was disquieting to some. But what, in all this, he was, as I say, concerned for was the Christian understanding, in faith, that GOD *himself*, and not another, had acted in love in the human scene. God himself had reached out to us: and God himself reaches out to us, in continuity with this, in the Spirit which is GOD at work in men to draw out of us if we will let him the Christlikeness that can be ours.

'He had a passion for unity', it was written of Charles Raven by his biographer, and they were the words with which Lampe explained the dedication of *God as Spirit*, the distillation of his life's work, to Raven's memory.

In that passion for the unity of things he was a prophetic figure for our own fragmented day, an authentic apostle in that appeal to the one true living GOD and in his assertion of a complementary truth which we need to hear and hear again in this day of false absolutes and idolatries which obliterate, as they surely do, humanity. Geoffrey is gone, and with so little notice taken by the official church of the report of its own Doctrine Commission, *Christian Believing*, and in it his fifteen classical pages; and who will now with quite the same persistence hold us to the truth that he there and constantly proclaimed and exhibited in his life: the truth that there is no infallibility, no indefectibility, except in God alone?

The living God addresses us. He speaks to us through our own humanity. 'We suppose', I quote Geoffrey Lampe on our great temptation, 'that when God speaks and acts humanity is bypassed' (*God as Spirit*, p. 205)—and it is not so.

That God in fact addresses *all* men, addressing them, from beyond themselves but in and through their humanity, with love and grace and beauty and in all their promptings towards truth, that GOD himself inspires us with the responsiveness we find within us, this he saw as life's meaning—and saw in Christ the focal point of this encounter, an encounter that is continually fresh, Christ, our Christ, 'belonging to the present more than to the past, and most of all to the future' (*Christian Believing*, p. 112). Here God's love meets us: and for the Christian the response must be a reaching out, exposed as we shall be, as fallible men, to the problems and tensions and ambiguities in which we get involved when we put ourselves in the service of love. There was for him no question about it at all: the churchman must be ready to be involved in political concern.

Here, surely, in his understanding of the way God treats them, was the source of his great respect for his fellow men and women, and of the respect they held him in: Geoffrey Lampe, as the Master of Caius College wrote of him, 'source of wisdom, good counsel and good company'. Here, certainly, was the spring of his optimism, his dismissiveness, as in a sermon remembered with great respect, so David Galilee tells me, in Sutton-in-the-Isle last Remembrance Day, of 'that defeatist cynicism which we indulge in far too much for our own good'.

There will be those here who heard him preach Mere's Commemoration Sermon to the University in St Bene't's Church on 15 April last. Few of those who heard it, or have read it since, will have failed to have an echo of it come to mind as they started a new University diary. He had known four years ago the surprise of learning of death as an immediate possibility, and had known what it was to say 'This cannot be so, for my diary is too full'. So, being Geoffrey, when given the choice he opted for Mere's theme of the preparation for death, and spoke of GOD, and, in effect, of life as gift.

> It seems, then, that to prepare against the fear of death we need to make the most of life: to enjoy life ourselves and to be thankful for it; to do our best to make it possible for other people to enjoy it more; to move through the enjoyment of life into enjoyment of God the source and giver of life, and to begin to experience that renewal of ourselves through his love which gives us the promise of fuller life to come.

So he had lived. So he died, clearsighted in the perspective of his dying, speaking out of his human incompleteness at the end, and by the way he died, of the God whose 'love is to be relied upon for ever' (*God as Spirit*, p. 205).

We give thanks, then, to God for Geoffrey Lampe, man of God. And we give thanks also, as he would have wished us to do in remembering him, for Elizabeth and what she gave to him for the true enjoyment of his life, that enjoyment which they shared so generously with others: and we pray that she may know God's love. And we remember their children, Nicolas and Celia, and the grandsons Gavin and Stefan who gave him such delight.

8

THE MERE'S COMMEMORATION SERMON

by G.W.H.L.

[Reprinted, by kind permission of Epworth Press and SCM Press, from Epworth Review, *Vol. 7, No. 3, 1980, where the sermon was first published; it was later included as Chapter 11 in* Explorations in Theology 8, *by G. W. H. Lampe, SCM Press 1981, pp. 130 ff]*

Preparation for Death

If the preacher of this sermon is to earn Mere's quarter of a mark, or three shillings and fourpence (which the university translates into 16p, having rounded it down, I reckon, by about two-thirds of a new penny—perhaps one of the minor effects of inflation), he is required 'to spend his matter in exciting the auditory to the diligent and reverent hearing and reading of the scripture', or 'in teaching due obedience of the subjects to their princes and of pupils to their tutors, of servants to their masters', or 'to exhort them to the relieving of the poor', or to 'exhort them to the daily preparation of death (which presumably means preparation *for* death), and not to fear death otherwise than scripture doth allow'. This present auditory seems to stand in less need than most people of excitement to the reading of scripture. That is how many of us spend the greater part of the working day. All of us, certainly, ought to do our best to relieve the poor; we do it in our various ways, and I do not think that any exhortation of mine on that duty would be particularly helpful. Few of us, on the other hand, are in a position to need advice on how to discharge the proper functions of either masters or servants, except in so far as we may all be said to be servants of the community. It is so long since I acted as a college tutor that it would be impertinent and improper for me to offer any teaching about the relation of pupils to their tutors; and I am unenthusiastic about obedience to those who, at the present moment at any rate, administer the government of our princes.

This leaves me with the subject of preparation against the fear of death, something with which we are all unquestionably concerned, since, whether we fear it or not, we shall all encounter death sooner or later and the time is never so very long. Indeed, it seems to be one of the curious features of life that the shorter the time that is left to us, according to our natural expectation of a full life-span, the faster it goes, so that days, months, years, all seem to end before we have scarcely realized that they have begun. At least, that is how it seems to me, though when I talked to someone recently about this phenomenon he depressed me not a little by saying: 'But mayn't this be parallel to the illusion of sitting in a moving train when in fact it's stationary and there's another train pulling out in the opposite direction? Are you quite sure that, instead of time speeding up, it isn't you slowing down?' Well, of course, that may be so; but in either case the effect is the same, and it is a reminder that the subject of death is always relevant, and for many of us, past middle age, by no means remote. It is a cliché to observe in this context that during the past century the subjects of death and sex have reversed their roles. The Victorians luxuriated in death but treated sex as taboo; our society does the opposite. Nevertheless, there was no lack of pornography in Victorian England, and at the present time there is an increasing amount of new writing on the subject of death, medical, sociological, philosophical, and religious—so much so that the constant assertion that the contemporary world has created a conspiracy of silence about death looks a little like the continuous clamour of those who call themselves the silent majority.

It is not only with death, however, that we are asked to concern ourselves today, but, more specifically, with 'fearing death', or, rather, with 'not fearing death'. I do not think most of us today do fear death in the way people feared it in Mere's time. Perhaps we do not fear death itself at all. It is possible, however, that others besides myself have found that whenever death becomes an immediate possibility instead of a remote dimly envisaged, terminal point lying far away at the other end of old age—when it suddenly appears as likely, at close quarters, in illness or accident or war—one feels not fear, but intense surprise, bewildering astonishment which can be demoralizing. It is the quite absurd feeling that this cannot be true, because, so one imagines, death is something that will happen to oneself, of course, *one day*, but it is only to other people that it actually comes here and now. One may even have the ridiculous notion that one cannot be going to die yet because one's diary is full of important things one is going to do for weeks and months ahead: a sort of crazy reversal of what ought, no doubt, to be a certain feeling of solemnity when we fill up a new diary at the start of the year—a recollection that the future is not our own possession to dispose of as we choose, and that it is well worth bearing in mind St James's warning that we ought to say, 'If the Lord will, we shall live and do this, or that'. Of course, there is another side to the full diary. Gustaf Aulén, who was producing highly fresh and original theology when he was in his late nineties, was said by the writer of a memoir to him to have always been so fully occupied that he simply never had the time to get round to dying. He was a man who made the very most of life, which is the best possible way to prepare for death.

It is, perhaps, against the surprise of being caught unawares by the prospect of death that we ought to be preparing, rather than against the fear of it. We need to be more realistic and less ready to delude ourselves with the notion that our own death and the ordinary routine of our daily existence are somehow incompatible and can never coincide. Yet there is some excuse for us if we fail to bring death into our normal calculations. To our ancestors, to the people of Mere's time, death was one of the most ordinary events in the everyday world. One's chances at birth of living to old age were small indeed. Deaths were always happening, among one's family and one's friends; there could be no pretence about that and no escape from it, and the frequency and inevitability of death and bereavement as present realities, not as something that will only happen one day, when we are old, were linked with a theology which could only make sense of all that wastage and sadness by thinking in terms of the direct action of God; in punishment for sin, in testing faith, or, as the burial service expressed it, in delivering our brethren out of the miseries of this sinful world. I have seen two memorials recording the entire wiping out of large families, one by one, within a few weeks or months, relentlessly, in times of plague in the seventeenth century. One is in Manchester Cathedral, the other at Bishop's Stortford. It was in that kind of world that Mere thought about fearing death, a world which very many of our fellow human beings still inhabit, partly through our own fault, but from which we in the West have been delivered by the progress of medical science and sanitary engineering—progress which, unless we destroy ourselves through political folly, surely makes this, our own age, the best time in all history to have lived in. Today we find it hard to imagine the state of mind of people who were at the same time powerless to prevent death and compelled to accommodate it within their theology as the direct act of God. We may think of Pusey, seeing his wife's death as divine judgment and making his dreadful resolve never to smile except in the company of children. As we now see such things, we realize that what was wanted was a proper drainage system for that house in Tom Quad. Good plumbing and much else on the material level save us from those forms of the fear of death. To a large extent we have been relieved, too, of the fear of dying. Medical science and skill have made the actual process of dying no longer terrible. We may be afraid of conditions which sometimes precede death: the kind of existence which all too many people have to live in geriatric wards. If so it is possible that death seems to us in those circumstances a blessing rather than a terror; we may think of euthanasia. However that may be, we are much less likely nowadays to have any reason to fear the process of dying than to be afraid of being kept physically alive when we have ceased to exist as fully human persons and we ought to be allowed to die.

The whole framework in which we think of the fear of death has changed since the time, in the astonishingly recent past, when to die before old age became unnatural, a result of accidents rather than sickness, and we came to think of death as the natural end of a full and completed life. We have begun to count on being able to grow old. This makes us take a very different view of death. For if one's life is complete, a finsihed whole, why should one be sad or frustrated at the prospect of death? Why, indeed, should one hope for life beyond death? Life begins and ends in mystery. We do not become conscious of ourselves as living people until we have already reached quite an advanced state of development and become quite sophisticated people. We become aware of ourselves as being here, not as having come here. There are, I believe, people who claim to have some kind of memory of being born, but I take leave to doubt that. At one time, not so long ago, we were not. Many people will say that at another time, not so far ahead, we shall again not be. Of course, if that should be true, those of us who hope and believe otherwise will not be disappointed, for there will be no 'we' to experience disappointment. It is perhaps rather comforting that what Professor Hick calls 'eschatological verification' can only work one way: it can only be positive. Either the hope of life beyond death will turn out to be true or we shall not be there to find it proved false.

If such people are right, we have our exits and our entrances, and what happens while we are on stage is our complete part in the play. Whether we act it well or not, we shall not come on again. We have done our part and made our contribution. If it has been a good contribution, then on this view we have no ground for complaint when it is time to make our exit. Value is not determined by, still less is it synonymous with, duration. I feel a good deal of sympathy with this attitude. We live in, and express ourselves through, our physical bodies, or, perhaps we ought to say, we live as our physical bodies. To depreciate the value of our bodily selves, as has been done in some religious traditions including some forms of Christianity, seems both futile and offensive to the Creator of the body. Yet I have no belief that the value of the body implies its indefinite duration, and the bodily life which is brought to an end by death seems to me to be enough. The body has by then played its part and completed its life-cycle. If there is life beyond death it seems that it must be life in a non-material and non-spatial dimension. Our life as persons, our expression of our personalities, and our relationships with others cannot then, as I see it, continue to be mediated in or as these physical machines which are to such a remarkably large extent devoted to the business of fuelling with food, drink and air, locomotion, and reproduction. A resurrection of the body in the literal sense of *resurrectio carnis* seems undesirable even were it conceivable; a transformation of the flesh into a bodily, yet spiritual and non-material, entity seems a self-contradictory notion which at the same time solves none of those admittedly grave problems of the mind/body relationship which are raised by the concept of bodiless personal existence. If, then, we can be content to find full value and satisfaction in our bodily

existence without hoping for its prolongation after the completion
of its natural term, might we not similarly be ready to accept death
as the end of ourselves as persons?

This is not necessarily an irreligious attitude. It was shared by
most of the Old Testament thinkers who combined the deepest
devotion to God and trust in his promises for the future of the
community with the conviction that 'the dead praise not thee, O
Lord, neither all they that go down into silence'. According to
Ecclesiasticus the hope of the individual should be to achieve a full
and successful and satisfying life, so that his good name and
reputation can live on after him and his children and his children's
children continue in some sense to represent him by perpetuating
his memory. It is not an unattractive idea for anyone whose life has
been full and satisfying. I have myself had an extremely happy life,
and so far as my own enjoyment goes I should, I think, be ready
when my time comes to be content to have had it without wanting
more. But this is basically a complacent attitude. The book
Ecclesiasticus is speaking for a privileged section of society: people
with achievements behind them, writers, poets, musicians, states-
men, 'leaders of the people by their counsel'. They are 'rich men
furnished with ability, living peaceably in their habitations'. You
can picture them in the ancient equivalents of lovely Georgian
country houses and cathedral precincts. The author knows very
well that there are others, 'who have no memorial, who are perished
as though they had never been'; and he is not interested in them, for
to look back on life in a spirit of complacent satisfaction is
essentially selfish. What about those who are perished as though
they had never been, who might, apparently, as well have never
lived? For the many whose lives are oppressed, unfree, handicap-
ped, sad, death must either be feared as the end of any possible
hope, or welcomed in sheer total despair, if this life is the whole
story. One may say that to encourage the unfortunate to hope for a
future life is to promise them pie in the sky, though a chance of pie
in the sky may perhaps be better than no pie at all; and when all has
been done that ought to be done, and that we ought to be doing, to
make life worth while and satisfying for all our neighbours, the fact
remains that not even social justice, the provision of health and
education, and the levelling of inequality, can eliminate all the
personal sadness, frustrations, alienation, and disappointments of
life, however much they improve the conditions in which it is lived.

Nor is it really good enough for us happier people to be simply satisfied with life as we've lived it. Is our part in the drama really so perfect? Is there no room for regret and can there be no scope for improvement? What about that curious sense, which I think grows much clearer with the years, that in so many of the most important aspects of life, especially in one's relations with other people, one is always just beginning, just now learning for the first time, just now unlearning mistakes, just being led to see things differently, making a fresh start? Isn't it the case that in spite of all the continuities that one can trace right through from childhood, and in spite of all the obvious ruts that one gets fixed in, one is continually becoming aware that one is a different person now from the person one used to be, and that one can confidently hope to be a different person again in the future from that which one is now: a better person, it is to be hoped, but, better or not, different. Life consists in change. It may be an illusion to think that one can look back on it as a static, completed, performance. We play many parts, one succeeding another, none complete, each adumbrating some fresh development. We are always on the way, almost growing up. I am not speaking of moral improvement or intellectual development so much as of the constant incompleteness and rudimentary state of our response to the outreach towards God—which involves our capacity to love and to respond to love in other people, mediating the love of God. All that really matters most in life is always deficient in us. We cannot possibly think that communion with God, that by which we truly live, is ever full, complete, and satisfying. That communion is what St Paul was talking about when he spoke of our inward man being renewed day by day. Renewal comes, or at least we experience renewal, in a very rudimentary way, and in fits and starts, however long we live this life. The people who are most conscious of its imperfection are the greatest of the saints. So, at the heart of our life there is unfulfilled hope, a promise and an assurance of the transformation of ourselves into the image of God in which, potentially, we have been created. That transformation cannot be completed in these few years of life; and if those years are all that there is for us, such glimpses of God as we now have are like a springtime without a summer to follow it. Here is real ground for fear, and we need trust and hope as our preparation against it.

Traditional Christianity would associate with death the fear of divine judgement. In so far as God's love touches us and moves us, there is always judgment, for love cannot but show up and condemn our selfishness and hates and greed and our total reversal of what should be the proper order of our priorities. And if the renewal of the inward man into Christlikeness is, as it must be, an infinte progress into the infinity of God, judgment can scarcely be other than infinite. But with infinite judgment there comes infinite forgiveness and infinite remaking. I have never been able to attach much meaning to that strange picture of a day when the books are opened, a balance struck, and the books closed again for ever. Nor can I see why judgment should be feared more after we die than in this present life. It may well be hard and painful, for much in us resists renewal and repels the love of God, but a judgment on selfishness which itself is transformation into love is a healing process, not something to be feared.

One fear seems to me impossible to remove until we come to know the truth about death: the fear of separation from those we love. There is the fear of bereavement for ourselves, and the fear of having as it were to desert those who depend on us. Of course, no one depends as much as we sometimes imagine. But this is a problem about the relation of time to eternity. It raises the question whether we can ever be separated from those with whom we are united (made one). I find it worth while to reflect on the attitude of some religious I have known. By consciously preparing for death and by holding their human friendships within the framework of their acceptance of the reality of death, they seem able in a most astonishing way to overcome separation and reduce it simply to the physical level. Those who have died just happen to be no longer visible.

It seems, then, that to prepare against the fear of death we need to make the most of life: to enjoy life ourselves and to be thankful for it; to do our best to make it possible for other people to enjoy it more; to move through the enjoyment of life into enjoyment of God the source and giver of life, and to begin to experience that renewal of ourselves through his love which gives us the promise of fuller life to come. To make the most of life is to come to be persuaded with St Paul 'that neither death, nor life, nor angels, nor principalities, nor powers, nor things present, nor things to come, nor height, nor depth, nor any other creature, shall be able to separate us from the love of God, which is in Christ Jesus our Lord'.